Phases

PHASES

The Spiritual Rhythms of Adult Life

Bernard Lievegoed

SOPHIA BOOKS
Rudolf Steiner Press
London

Translated by H.S. Lake

Sophia Books
Rudolf Steiner Press
51 Queen Caroline Street
London W6 9QL

First edition 1979, Pharos Books (Rudolf Steiner Press), London
Second edition 1982, Pharos Books
Third edition 1979, Rudolf Steiner Press; reprinted 1993
This edition 1997
(Sophia Books is an imprint of Rudolf Steiner Press)

Originally published by Lemniscaat, Rotterdam in 1976 under the title
De levensloop van de mens

A catalogue record for this book is available from the British Library

ISBN 1 85584 056 1

Cover by Andrew Morgan
Typeset by DP Photosetting, Aylesbury, Bucks
Printed and bound in Great Britain by Cromwell Press Limited, Wiltshire

Contents

Preface

This book is the result of many conversations that I have had over the years with a wide variety of people who were struggling to understand their own lives or, in some cases, the lives of others.

Through popular scientific writing and through the media of radio and television, many people have been brought into contact with frequently contradictory views of human nature put forward by different schools of thought in psychology and psychiatry. Creating order in this chaos of conflicting ideas can have a liberating effect.

In this work I have tried to create such order starting from a personalistic point of view, so that man is seen as a physical being (the biological image of man), as a psyche (the psychological image of man), and as a spirit being (the biographical image of man). The path of an individual's life (his biography) can only be appreciated fully as a unique personal 'work of art' if these three viewpoints are combined to form a single image.

This book gives a general account of the phases in a human being's life, and the characteristic, ever-changing problems and opportunities that they bring. At the same time, certain critical stages and situations in people's lives are discussed, along with the problems associated with them. In this way it is hoped that this book will offer the reader a basis for insight into the course of his own life and an understanding of the biographical development of others.

B.L.

Introduction

Working with the problems of human development and of biography has occupied a central place in my life for over 40 years. In my work in remedial education and child psychiatry the important question was of the meaning of early disturbances in the patient's life taken as a whole. In the psychotherapy of adolescents and adults it was the search for the leitmotiv which guided the entire span of life from childhood to old age. Later, in youth work and education for young unskilled factory workers, and in the development of vocational training, the question became: what must be done *now* in order to lay the foundations for the future so that new problems in later life can be met creatively?

Later still, 'the phases of human development' became a central part of my work with managers and in organizations. Finally, the transition from education by others to self-education in an *éducation permanente* became a basic feature of the first-year course at the Free College at Driebergen (Holland).

Throughout my work I have been struck by the fruitfulness of placing the problems of the moment into the larger context of the totality of human life. The present is, after all, determined equally by past causal factors and by future directions. Whereas causal factors are established fact, only the prospects — the future — leave the social worker or the therapist a degree of freedom. It is often more important to help a person define a new future than to linger on a past which cannot be altered.

Many times during these 40 years I have felt the urge to commit to paper the experiences gained from this involvement with the course of human life. However, each time, a feeling that I was not yet ready made me postpone it, seemingly for another decade or so. Meanwhile the feeling of not being prepared for the magnitude of the task has not grown less: on the contrary. But another sober fact, connected with the course of my own life, has finally persuaded me to go ahead and write this book; when you reach the age of 70, it is a matter of now or never. I hope, therefore, that this book, with all its shortcomings, will be read as the life-work of a psychiatrist-cum-social-worker.

Any writer must see before him a particular public to which he wishes to address himself. For a thesis this may be a critical faculty board, for an article it may be his colleagues. In either case, the first thing one is likely to do is to view one's own contribution in the light of the state of the science at the moment of writing. At this stage one then has to balance the ideal of thoroughness against the unattractiveness of an argument which staggers forward on crutches of footnotes. The public that I see before me as I write is the audience of my many courses and lectures, ranging from works foremen to university graduates, and they all had one thing in common: they had enquiring minds, and above all they were interested in the problems of how their own lives were developing and what meaning their lives had.

This work is not written from the viewpoint of 'objective' behavioural science as this would exclude what happens inside us, the meanings and intentions we give to life. It is precisely what goes on inside the behavioural scientist's 'black box', inside us, which is of interest. The course of human life is, after all, not something that can be described as a programmed succession of chemical reactions or likened to the fate of a ball-point pen from the moment when it leaves the factory until the moment at which— having been used by various owners—it ends up in the waste-paper basket.

In the first place the course of human life has a biological aspect which can be described from the outside in its ascendancy and decline. It also has a psychological aspect, experienced in thoughts, feelings and impulses of the will. And it has a spiritual aspect of individuation, of value choice, of meaning, and of realizing some amount of ego potential. It is these latter psychological and spiritual aspects which concern us most, for *that is what we are* as humans, as contrasted with zoological objects. It is these parts of our life which I will focus on primarily.

In order to study these aspects of life it is necessary to make introspection a method of research. However, in saying this, I mean an introspection exercised with just as much discipline as mathematical thinking. Systematic daily introspection, tested critically against observations, values and norms, needs to be exercised in order to give our experiences order. People find it quite normal that years of concentration and study are necessary before it becomes possible to see through a problem of higher mathematics. The layman who claims 'I've had a quick look at it myself and it was rubbish' is not taken seriously, and rightly so. The same applies to the knowledge that may be gained through introspection and through introspective discussion with others. In the past people talked of concentration, meditation and contemplation, but nowadays the talk is more of introspection and empathic understanding. In reality this last is impossible without systematic con-centration and meditational involvement with inner phenomena. And for that it is necessary to build up a conscious and rich inner life. It is from this perspective that I have written this work.

As regards his innermost psyche modern man, in the materialistic society of today, finds he has embarked on a journey through the desert. His thirst can be quenched only by repeated attention to the replenishing concepts and feelings that make sense of his existence and put the totality of his own humanity in a human as well as in a spiritual world of ethical and aesthetic values. An understanding of the phases of human life can become a path through the desert and can begin to give meaning to existence.

The earliest description of the phases of human life is to be found in the Chinese proverb 'Human life consists of three phases: 20 years for learning, 20 years for fighting, and 20 years for attaining wisdom.'

If in this book the reader finds something of the essence of this Chinese proverb, then one of its aims will have been achieved.

Chapter One

Surveying the Terrain

1. Defining the Problem

Today it is possible to discern a growing interest in questions of man's inner life. It has already been suggested in the Introduction that the behavioural scientists' 'black box' is no longer accepted as something which cannot be known, purely and simply because we ourselves *are* the black box, and because we want to be able to deal with ourselves consciously, for which we require an understanding of what goes on inside us. This has led to the development, alongside 'academic psychology', of a second kind of psychology, which has arisen largely from the observation of the mentally ill.

This development began towards the end of the last century in Freudian psychoanalysis and runs via Adler, Jung and Frankl to Assagioli (to confine ourselves for the moment to its European representatives). At the same time there arose an interest in a psychology of development which was not psychoanalytical, associated with names such as Charlotte Bühler, Rümke, Künkel, Guardini, Martha Moers, Andriessen, etc. Only within the last few years have these two schools begun to interact with each other to their mutual benefit.

Many people seek a guide to their experiences of a confusing inner world. This inner world may contain elements from a subconscious world full of unassimilated experiences of life, of deeply-felt emotions, drives and archetypes. They penetrate our daily consciousness through the world of dreams or through frightening experiences which may upset our entire inner equilibrium.

It is clear that the development of western civilization has now progressed to a point at which it crosses the threshold between 'normal' consciousness and the subconscious. Collective emotions and 'invasions' have always broken through the surface at critical moments in history, securing an outlet in revolutions and wars. But now they are recognized for what they are, and the question is being asked: how can we handle such forces so that they do not, now that the destructive power of our weapons has become so great, lead us into world catastrophe?

But there is also a crossing of a threshold in another direction. Increasing numbers of philosophers, psychologists and psychiatrists are pointing out that besides a subconscious, the human being also has a higher consciousness, out of which he can find values, norms and meanings which may reveal the future in a purposeful way. This direction or purpose, which can pervade the course of life as a leitmotiv, can give the strength which steers the emotions and invasions into non-destructive paths.

The materialism which reached its zenith during the second half of the last century was able to invest these values, norms and objectives with nothing more than a simulated existence, an illusion, a projection, a sublimation. They were defined as castles in the air built by a 'naked ape' who thought himself a man.

So there came into being a form of psychoanalysis which divided these 'higher things' and took visible pleasure in doing so. But every one-sided view gives rise to its counterpart, and as the opposite pole to psychoanalysis there developed a psychosynthesis which sees the true essence of humanity in a higher *ego*, which, like a lode-star, shines over the whole territory of the mind. On the one hand we have animal man, driven by the principle of desires to be satisfied. On the other we have spiritual man, with his development towards an individual future in which meaning is given to love and pain, to receiving and sacrificing. The first of these thresholds was crossed in the early years of this century, the second after the middle of the century.

Unmoved by these inner, turbulent developments, developmental psychologists sought for the laws governing the course of human life, and it will not be easy in this book to reveal the coherence of these many paths. This is partly because not only did the developmental psychologists take scant notice of the battle for the image of the inner being being fought by researchers calling themselves analytical, synthetic or existentialist, but these last, too, developed their images of man and their therapies without paying much attention to the course of human biography.

Thus therapies were created based on the encounters between therapists and problems of a particular phase of life, and these were then proclaimed as valid for all ages. This emerged most clearly in the conflict between Freud and Jung: Freud with his practice of younger people with their manifest sexual complexes, and Jung with older people in whom the fear of death and the sense of having failed to break through to a spiritual ideal played a central part.

Since the 1950s the need for a complete image of man, taking into account everyday consciousness, a subconscious and a higher consciousness has grown in both America and Europe. This has also meant an increasing need for guidance in problems associated with inner development. The field is covered by individual psychiatrists, psychotherapists and counsellors (in the USA), together with institutions providing group training facilities and enthusiastic but not all equally expert amateurs. Their backgrounds may vary, but they are all in search of a personalistic approach to problems of human relations, marriage, and blocked development.

A completely different group seeks a guide for an inner path of development in search of their own higher ego in a spiritual world, or a merging with some mystical oneness through ancient oriental mysticism.

Among the first group there are those who wish to make their way through a systematic training of thinking, feeling and willing and the development of imaginative, inspirative and intuitive faculties. In Rudolf Steiner they find a guide who can teach them how they can place these faculties at the service of humanity, in education, agriculture, and medicine. And finally there are a number of people, primarily young, who find the path of systematic development too slow, and who believe that they will be able to push on through to a higher consciousness with the aid of chemistry. They certainly experience the crossing of a threshold, but they then find themselves in a twilight area in which they become acquainted with experiences that are highly emotional for the individual person but which they cannot use further. On the contrary, we see them sliding ever further into alienation or even taking refuge in hard drugs.

For many people these phenomena are no more than what they read in books or newspapers. They are interested in their own lives or in those of their fellows. For them the more phenomenological descriptions of the course of human life will be important. Especially if at the same time attention is drawn to critical points in the biography and the kinds of problems which play a part in such crises, so that the difficult periods in their own lives may be seen as part of a meaningful whole.

With this description the ingredients of this book have already been hinted at. To list them one by one, they are: a phenomenological description of the course of human life; the analysis of a biological, a psychological and a spiritual life-path; a discussion of images of man and schools of thought in therapy that may give this life-path a background; the indication of possible ways of avoiding or curing disturbances in the course of one's life; and in that connection, an aid in the crossing of the threshold which we must all accomplish after our forties.

2. Human Development

'Development' is a term used to indicate a number of directed changes within a period of time. In my book *The Developing Organization* (pp. 39–47) I have discussed the concept of development at some length. There I distinguished between 'change', 'growth', and 'development'.

The term 'change' tells us merely that nothing is static and that everything moves in the stream of time. It is only when there is some system behind the change that it becomes interesting; it is then possible to speak of laws such as those described by the sciences. 'Growth' is a systematic change in which a quantitative increase in number, size or weight of a given element takes place within the same system. A crystal grows in weight and dimensions, a city grows in area and population, a club grows in membership, and so on.

'Development' is growth in which structural changes occur at critical points throughout the system. According to Charlotte Bühler, development is a change which takes place in one direction, governed by laws of maturation.

'Development is fundamentally biological,' says Dale Harris in *The Concept of Development*. Growing quantitatively, an organism reaches a limit beyond which its original simple structure is no longer capable of maintaining it. Continued growth then means the disintegration of the organism (in the form of biological death, for example), or, alternatively, a reordering of its internal structure so that control can be maintained despite the organism's increased size.

Development takes place even in the simplest of living organisms. Referring to this simple development, Dale Harris speaks of 'blueprinted growth'. It begins with a repeated process of cell-division and differentiation to form organs, leading to the overall form which the organism is to take. This is the maturation stage. There then follows a stage of equilibrium between maturation and decline, the phase in which the adult organism functions as such. Finally there is a third stage in which decline increasingly predominates until death intervenes.

In this process, plants grow from seed to stem and leaf and finally to flower and seed, often within the annual cycle. In perennial plants the process repeats itself in an enduring skeleton which sends out new shoots each year.

Animals have the same life cycle of maturation — equilibrium — decline, although each species has its own span of life. We say that animal life is determined *chronotypically*. Mice live for between a year and a half and two years; a dog may live to be 12 or 15; man's life-span, once 'three-score years and ten', is now somewhat more than that.

If we consider the structure of an organism, a development process is by definition discontinuous. Development is growth from structural crisis to structural crisis. Here again we can distinguish several stages.

(a) *Growth of the entire organism* (or of parts of it).

(b) *Differentiation and organ formation.* Functions initially fulfilled equally throughout the system are now concentrated and refined in subsystems (organs).

(c) *Hierarchization.* Some organs take on the function of governing others. This is also known as 'hierarchical integration'.

(d) *Integration.* A new system is formed, and the organism as a whole now functions with a higher degree of complexity and at a higher level.

Biological development is always directed *finally*. Every living thing develops *towards an end*, towards the predetermined form of the adult organism. Maturation, equilibrium and decline all play a part. This rule applies to all living organisms, including man, whose cycle of equilibrium and situations between maturation and decline we shall examine later.

So far we have been on safe, familiar ground. However in man, a number of developments take place at the same time; they all have their own patterns, but each influences the other. These three development patterns may be termed as follows:

biological development
psychological development
spiritual development

As soon as we start talking about psychological and spiritual development we find ourselves in an area of controversy. The various different schools of thought are still engaged in a conflict which is often fought with each side claiming absolute right, discriminating against every other opinion or approach than their own. The behavioural sciences and depth psychology on the one hand and experimental sensory psychology and psychotherapy on the other have no common ground on which they can meet.

As regards images of man and therapeutic schools of thought we may make the following observations. The Viennese psychiatrist Frankl refers to the reduced images of man, presented by biology, psychology and sociology. These he calls biologisms (man is a biological object, fashioned by genetics), psychologisms (man is fashioned by his education), and sociologisms (man is shaped by his environment or class). These reduced images of man are blind to the spiritual in man as a quality in itself. The complete man whom Frankl seeks is not governed and ruled by blind drives or desires, nor is he moulded by his upbringing, education and surroundings. To the contrary, he seeks his own way *in spite of* all these. The way which he seeks incorporates joy and sorrow, love and pain, as meaningful aspects of a path of development towards achieving complete humanity.

Thirty years ago I wrote *Ontwikkelingsfasen van het kind* (The Development Phases of the Child). There I included a small diagram of the image of man underlying the book, which was written for parents and educators.

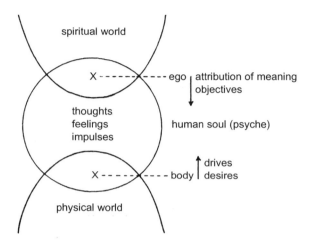

This image shows a polarity in the human soul (the psyche, expressing itself in thoughts, feelings and impulses, with our day-to-day ego at its centre). On the one hand there is the pole of physicality, from which drives and desires become discernible in the soul. On the other hand, there is the spiritual pole, where the soul is within the field of the mind, in a real divine-spiritual world. Here, through self-awareness and in the attribution of meaning to life, the true ego of man as a spiritual being is observable in the soul.

For the benefit of the following discussion I would add to this that thinking is most directly connected with the world of the spirit, while willing is most closely involved in the physical world of the body. Feeling is in the middle, and is for many people the true quality of the psyche.

During the middle phase of life, as we shall see in the following chapters, thinking, feeling and willing are indi-vidualized by the higher ego so that they become the 'sen-tient soul', the 'intellectual soul', and the 'consciousness soul'. Having been developed one after the other, these give each phase of life its own colour. In the final phase of life the ego can have a further effect on thoughts, feelings and impulses, so that the life of the sentient soul leads to imagination, the life of the intellectual soul results in inspiration, and the life of the consciousness soul produces intuition (see the final chapter).

In this book I shall describe the growth and development to adulthood and maturity. To some extent, this development comes about naturally, but its completion can only take place if we consciously wish to carry it through to the finish. Education from outside is then supplemented by self-education from within, sometimes called a path of inner development. It is only thus that the development of thought, feeling and willing can be completed, and only then that man unfolds fully to become what he *can* become. Cleverness grows in stature to become wisdom, the ability to communicate becomes kindness, and self-assurance becomes confidence.

3. The Spiritual Element in the Human Being

In our daily experience we encounter, as already described, drives and desires, which arise from the physical-biological sphere, and spiritual aims and norms, which come from our spiritual self or higher ego.

In other words, two force-fields act upon each other continuously in the human soul. One comes from the physical area, where desires and their satisfaction alternate, and the other comes from the spiritual area, where the conscious ego alternately directs the soul outwards at the world and inwards at itself. Extroversion and introversion alternate as do desire and satisfaction.

In extroversion the psyche or soul is focused through the senses at the world outside, experiencing colours and shapes, ecstasy and agony, sympathy and antipathy. In introversion the soul is turned inwards upon its own inner world. This is a world of experience in which memories come to the fore, in which we think, feel and will. Here, alongside thought, experience and ambition fill the soul, as long as the soul is conscious (awake). We may accept, I think, that depth psychology has shown that the soul also remains active in the unconscious and half-conscious sleep and dream state. The human spirit is experienced as our own ego or higher ego, which both consciously and unconsciously gives direction to our biography. The spirit is aimed at the objective of life; it is always directed *finally*. In the soul this objective may be experienced as a calling, thought as a life-plan, or willed as a life-path.

Just as in the biological sphere desire and satisfaction belong together as opposite poles, so, in the spirit, are objective and fulfilment related. An aim in life can be fulfilled gradually. Fulfilment is an existential experience of happiness or joy which does not—unlike the satisfaction of a desire—demand new satisfaction. (In his book *Levenstijdperken van de man*—The Stages of Man's Life—Rümke has already pointed out the essential difference between the satisfaction of desires and life fulfilment.)

If the ego is actively turned outwards, it expresses itself in creativity. *Creativity is activity by the mind in the world.* The mind, or spirit, can manifest itself in art, science or scholarship, or social activity. In creativity we encounter something of the individuality of a person. We recognize the composer in his music, the great scholar in his method and the leader in creative social deeds.

Diametrically opposed to creativity we find *wisdom*. Wisdom comes not from outward-directed activity, but from being able to wait and see, from *restraint*, from *active peace of mind*. Youth has little patience: things must happen *now*. A wise person has learnt that insight comes if it is not hurried, that everything needs time. Wisdom is based on *inspiration,* and inspiration, literally, means 'breathing in'. Wisdom is breathing in, filling oneself with spirit, with norms and values, with meaning, with humanity and super-humanity — with faith, hope, and charity.

Biological development takes place in the polarity of *maturation and decline*

Development of the psyche (or soul) takes place in the polarity of *extroversion and introversion*

Spiritual development takes place in the polarity between *creativity and wisdom.*

In youth and during the expansive period of adulthood, creativity plays the major role in spiritual development. In the *second half of life* this role is taken over by wisdom.

The spirit is at once creativity *and* wisdom. Hence the soul is at once extroversion and introversion, the expiration *and* the inspiration of the world, diastole and systole.

Both artists and scientists know that inspiration cannot be forced. Inspiration comes only where in the struggle for active peace of mind the direct result is pushed into the background. *Active peace of mind* is brought about by putting the emotions to rest, by imposing silence on all associative thoughts and renouncing all desired results. It is the most difficult of all things for a man to achieve. If inspiration manifests itself in the soul, then that is the expression of its most essential expressiveness. If inspiration comes, its effect on extrovert minds is creativity; the introvert mind, on the other hand, converts it into wisdom.

In saying that, I use the term 'wisdom' to cover not only the wisdom of elevated philosophical systems, but also, more importantly, the *wisdom of life* which may be found in every rank and class and degree of learning. I have found wisdom on the shop floor just as often as in the boardroom. And the same, of course, goes for lack of wisdom! In the second half of life lack of wisdom always arises from being unable to wait, an incapacity to see things in perspective which leads to hasty decisions, which in turn finally leads to disaster. Every dictator (and creativity is one thing that every dictator must be admitted to have) ultimately falls because of his own obstinacy, because he does not know when to stop.

The polarities to which I have referred all have a *middle*; it is not merely an apparently stationary equilibrium of two polar forces, but it is itself an *active force in man*. It is, indeed, the essence of human existence.

Between biological growth and decline there is a state of *good health*, between psychological extroversion and introversion there is a state of *peace of mind*, and between spiritual creativity and wisdom there is human happiness, *fulfilment*.

Each of the three polarities thus has a threefold nature:

Growing .... *Good health* .... *Decline*
Extroversion ..... *Peace of mind* .... *Introversion*
Creativity .... *Fulfilment* .... *Wisdom*

Good health, peace of mind and happiness are the fruits of a stable development. I shall go into greater detail on this point especially in the chapter on psychotherapy. With the phenomenological descriptions of the human life-path we shall further examine the fields of tension referred to above. They play very different roles in various phases of our lives.

In Chapter Six we shall look at the images of man which are or have been current in our society. We shall see that each of these images lays the emphasis on biological development, on psychological development, or on spiritual development. My own view is that all three provide legitimate data on the human life-path. It is only when we consider *all three* in their interaction that the picture becomes more complete.

4. The Images of Man

By way of introduction to the description of the human life-path I will now briefly describe a number of images of man which are discussed at greater length in Chapter Six. In principle there are four possible images of man:

1. The Mechanistic-materialistic Image of Man

This was the ideal of the end of the nineteenth century: *l'homme machine* or *der Mensch als Industrie-Palast*, a picture which in the days of my youth still used to hang in the display cases at the chemist's. There, man was seen as the sum of a number of machine components: the brain was a telephone exchange, the heart a pumping-station, the digestive system a furnace, and the windpipe a chimney from which clouds of smoke emerged. As a whole, this primitive image of man has been abandoned, though parts of it continue to turn up from time to time. The heart as a pumping-station is one such persistent image.

The modern 'medical model' may be said to be the transition from the mechanistic to the chemical image of man. Chemical processes in the body must be fed, controlled or influenced by chemical substances. This leads to a school of thought devoted to curing ailments by chemical means, and hence also to the modern pharmaceutical industry, producing such chemicals by the train-load and pouring them down the collective throat of western mankind.

2. The Biological Image of Man

This is composed, in the first place, of the image of man created by the biochemists. Here, *every* human expression is a result of complex, chemical processes — not only the chemical processes of digestion, or the electrochemical processes of the brain, but also the mental processes such as thinking, feeling and willing. There is no room in this image of man for spiritual values and standards, even though the biochemists themselves use values and standards continuously.

Apart from this biochemically oriented picture, the biological image of man also contains a *zoological* picture, composed chiefly of hereditary factors and supported by the biochemists in their research into the molecular structure of genetic material. Here, man is 'no more than' the highest mammal, the result of random mutations and selection. The tiny area of comparability of chimpanzee and human behaviour is joyfully enlarged upon by people who are apparently blind to the immeasurably vast areas of difference.

Adherents of the biological image of man may be classed as *nativists*. They would reduce everything to heredity and genetics. They have in common that they defend their views aggressively and heap scorn on those of unlike persuasion.

3. The Psychological Image of Man

Here attention is focused principally on the psyche, on the mental processes of man. To begin with, the behavioural sciences developed, starting from the consideration that whatever goes on inside a person can only be known through subjective descriptions, whereas behaviour can be established objectively and is therefore susceptible to research. If we suppose that the mind is a black box, then what goes in (the stimulus) and what comes out (the reaction) can be observed and recorded. So arose behaviourism, the theory of behaviour, and stimulus-response psychology.

In empiricism this image of man was applied to education and upbringing. On the basis of experience with underfed pigeons and rats a technique of training and indoctrination was developed which was then transferred to human processes. This led to the now familiar programmes of programmed teaching and multiple-choice examinations. The empiricists take practically no account of inherited aptitude, which, according to them, is so diverse and open that in practice behaviour is determined by environmental factors (culture and upbringing). At present the behavioural sciences in sociology, psychology and economics exercise a dominant influence, though the zenith of this intellectual fashion has passed.

4. The Personalistic-spiritual Image of Man

Here the stress is laid on the importance of the higher ego in man, on the person who states his aims, takes decisions, finds and determines values and standards, and is gradually revealed in the thread which runs through the entire biography.

Artists, and particularly the writers of biographies, make their subject the study and description of the development of human personality in wisdom or folly, level-headedness or uncontrollability, health or sickness. The results have varied from the level of penny thrillers to milestones in world literature. But until a few decades ago this was literature and not science. Then an increasing number of psychologists and educators began to experience the one-sidedness and poverty of behavioural science and sought to include the spiritual development of man in arriving at an understanding of man and his social actions. From this there emerged educational schools of thought which no longer wished to see learning or teaching as training and indoctrination with previously determined programmes, but which elevated concepts like self-discovery, self-development and self-realization to educational objectives, embracing Heraclitus' pronouncement that 'upbringing is not filling a bucket, but lighting an open fire'.

After 1945 a new branch of psychology arose: humanistic psychology, concerned with the description of and research into human personality in its expression and development, and with the possibilities, referred to above, of active peace of mind, creativity and wisdom. In fields that had hitherto been dominated by biology and the behavioural sciences, new concepts came to the fore such as ecological equilibrium and optimal well-being instead of maximum standards of living. This development has now become so clearly visible and has brought about such revolutionary changes in our value priorities that it is almost possible to speak in terms of a spiritual-social revolution, probably *the* revolution of the twentieth century!

This brief description, I hope, will be sufficient to enable the reader to follow my discussion of the human life-path itself. In Chapter Six these images of man will be dealt with in greater detail.

5. The Division of Life into Phases

'Every period of life has its own point, its own purpose. To find it and accept it is one of the most vital problems relating to life.'
(Erich Stern)

The division of the human life-path into phases has been a controversial point for some time. One view is that there *are* no phases, and that every development is a gradual sliding from condition to condition, indiscernible if one follows closely the biography from day to day. Furthermore, such a thing as the crisis of puberty, described by development psychologists, is viewed as an artificial, culturally determined affair, resulting from the way in which western culture views sexual and social maturation.

The point about gradual change, observed at very short intervals, has little to do with the existence of childhood, youth and adulthood. It is like the transition from day into night; if we follow it by the minute we cannot say, at any one moment, that the day has ended and the night begun. Nevertheless, there comes a time when it is completely dark; it is night, and we can contrast night and day. So, too, we cannot identify one particular day as the instant at which the transition from youth to adulthood takes place; yet there comes a time when the individual involved has acquired so many adult characteristics and shed so many of the characteristics of youth that we can speak of that person having attained adulthood (albeit a passing form thereof).

The other, more sociological argument, which claims cultural shaping of the so-called phases of life, has some basis in fact. For example, the *way in which* puberty is experienced in the mind is strongly dependent upon a number of external factors. In the first place, it is dependent on the demands made upon an adolescent. For example, the child of an intellectual family in Britain is likely to go through a different kind of stress at his public school than a Kikuyu boy in Kenya being initiated into adult male society having passed through puberty. But the fact that both have reached the stage at which they must round off their childhood and reorientate themselves in the world about them is a clear indication of a transition from one phase in life to the next.

Biological development, particularly during the first half of one's life, is an important basis for mental and spiritual reorientation. In the second half of life it is the spiritual personality which increasingly takes over this task by setting targets and making normative choices. As we shall see, it is precisely after the forties, when the biological line of life has begun to decline, that it becomes important to break free of biological evolution and aspire to increased mental and spiritual performance.

Where the body, soul and spirit of a man function as one unit, there is never any question of only one of these having an influence, but of a shifting balance between the three. And it is precisely this shifting balance which makes transitions fluent and yet clearly perceptible — providing, of course, we *want* to perceive them.

I shall now turn to a number of those who have in the past investigated the phases of human life, after which I shall explain the basis for my own choices.

There are schemata where the human life-path is divided into regular periods of seven, 14 or 21 years, and there are schemata which divide our lives into five, seven or nine phases. The differences between these views are, however, less than one might imagine. In the first place, the important turning-points in the biography coincide in virtually all schemata, and for the rest the division is dependent on secondary criteria.

The oldest schema to have an influence on western culture is the Greek, which divides life into hebdomads, ten phases of seven years. Ptolemy's view, however, went against those of his contemporaries by describing irregular phases of life, each of which came under the influence of one of the planets (Lauer: *Der menschliche Lebenslauf*—The Course of Human Life).

The Romans talked of five phases of life:

0–15 years, *pueritia* (early childhood and the latent period of the early school years)
15–25 years, *adulescentia*
25–40 years, *iuventus* (first adulthood)
40–55 years, *virilitas* (second adulthood)
55 and older, *senectus* (old age).

Of Dutch authors, *Rümke* endorses the Roman view, though he adds a *praesenium* from 55 to 65, and his old age starts at 65.

Watering, according to Rümke, follows the Greeks by distinguishing between ten phases of seven years:

0–7 years, the period of fantasy life
7–14 years, the period of imaginative life
14–21 years, puberty and adolescence
21–28 years, discovering and controlling the basis of one's life
28–35 years, consolidating and confirming that basis once found

35–42 years, second puberty (reorientation with regard to one's calling in life)
42–49 years, the manic depressive period
49–56 years, the struggle against one's own decline
56–63 years, maturity of thought
63–70 years, second childhood — if the transition is consciously accepted, it may lead again to a new high point.

Wijngaarden has distinguished between three main phases:

0–18 years, *acquaintance* with the inner and outer world
18–42 years, *acceptance* of the inner and outer world
42–death, *reflection* on the inner and outer world.

Andriessen discusses not so much the phases of life in terms of calendar years as the principles which determine the nature of the phases of life. At this point it may be observed that all writers who have thought about phases of life and have investigated them are more or less explicit personalists.

From the standpoint of Freud's psychoanalysis much has been written about development psychology, but there the development ends either at the sixth or at the fourteenth year of life, after which the individual is supposed to develop no further because from this orientation development can come only from the life of biological desires, and the mental person is no more than a 'superstructure' built on such desires: the id.

Later a number of Freud's followers paid more attention to the ego itself — not merely as a product of the id. Here there is talk of an individual's ego-aptitude, which is present from the very beginning and does not arise out of the id (Erikson and others).

The best known of woman writers on the human life-path is Charlotte Bühler. She again distinguishes between five phases of life which are identical to those of Rümke. More important than the division into periods of years, however, is Charlotte Bühler's view that each individual has a leit-motiv directed at a target and the selection of a way towards that target. In Charlotte Bühler's view of things, developments during an individual's life take place depending on which of a number of basic biological drives is dominant. These are:

1. Satisfaction of *needs*
2. Limiting *self-accommodation* by self-determination from within; otherwise the regulation of the individual's life
3. Maintenance of *inner order* by which continuity is made possible (Charlotte Bühler herself refers to genuine conscience, which provides guidance 'through the true self')
4. *Creative expansion.*

In the various phases of life these basic drives have varying influence.

Charlotte Bühler further builds up her developmental possibilities around the polarity of *vitality* (the biological-physical aspect of man) and *mentality* (the spiritual and mental aspect of man, directed towards the completion of the life task). She sees two lines of development in inter-action — a biological and a mental and spiritual development. The basic drives work from within the biological person, the motives from within the spiritual person.

In this way the psychological side of the human life-path becomes the 'motivation-path'. Each life has a primary intention: the leitmotiv or guiding motive. Alongside the biological life-path of building — equilibrium, decline, death — she sets a biographic life-path scheme of getting under way — seeking and trying, the final track, zenith, drawing up the balance and decline.

In my later discussion of the phases of life we shall see that my own approach to the life-path shows two possible zeniths of two completely different qualities.

Charlotte Bühler herself feels that with her polarity between vitality and mentality she has not found a more accurate description of the human life-path. In her thinking the concept of mentality is not sharply defined. At one moment it may tend to be the totality of the psychological personality, the next it tends to be more the ego, of which she says that from as early as the second year of life it consciously and powerfully pushes *its own* targets, in direct contradiction to its surroundings, while at the same time, even at this early stage, the function of conscience is beginning.

The human life-path will have to be described as a function of a trinity of body, psyche and spirit, in which the psyche is the ever-changing constellation of thoughts, feelings and impulses brought about by biological developments on the one hand and by spiritual developments (through the stating of a self-determining target of life) on the other. This target of life then leads, depending on the individual biography, to a greater or lesser degree of life-fulfilment, which is experienced in the soul. Charlotte Bühler calls fulfilment the successful realization of life values.

Chorus (*Psychologie van de menselijke levensloop* — Psychology of the Course of Human Life) is an explicit personalist. For him, the *biographic* method of research stands diametrically opposite the scientific. The former individualizes, the latter generalizes.

The biographic method approaches the individual along his own life-path. It examines in detail man's exceptional position with regard to the higher mammals and confirms our view of the early birth of the human baby: 'the end of the first year would be the time of human birth if man were only a mammal'. Pregnancy would then have to be a year longer (the Basle zoologist Adolf Portmann also speaks of man as having a 'physiological premature birth'). The biographic method states that every phase has a shape of its own—that it has its own meaning and cannot be replaced by any other.

A particular contribution to our understanding of the human life-path has been made by the philosopher Guardini. His book *Die Lebensalter* (The Periods of Life) ought to have a place in everyone's library. Although it can easily be read in an evening, it contains a wealth of carefully formulated human wisdom and intimate perception. Here are a few sentences from this little work:

> Man characterizes himself again and again, and still it is always the same man living in each phase. The person is conscious of himself and has to account for the phases in question. Each phase has its own nature, which can be deduced neither from the preceding nor from the subsequent one. The values (in people) form a picture, a configuration and they do so by being determined by a dominating value centre [*Wertmitte*]. The child is in the world not merely in order that he may become adult, but also, and primarily, in order that he may himself be a child and, as a child, a part of mankind. For mankind comprises all living men, in whatever phase of their lives they may be—thus the true child is no less a part of mankind than the true adult.

For each phase, Guardini looks for the dominant factor— the 'centre of gravity', the *Wermitte*. The phases which he describes are the following:

1. Life in the womb, birth and childhood
2. The crisis of the years of maturation (puberty)
3. The young person (adolescence)
4. The crisis of experience (the transition from adolescence to expansionary adulthood)
5. The emancipated man (the thirties)
6. The crisis of limitations (the beginning of the forties)
7. The sobered man

8. The crisis of new freedom
9. The wise man.

It is conspicuous that Guardini focuses his attention first and foremost on the important transitions between phases of life. For all these phases, the following applies: *'Life consists not in a joined series of loose parts, but is a single whole which is present at any given moment of its course.* Thus its end has an effect throughout life, namely, the fact that the light of life shall dim and one day be extinguished; that everything that happens is moving towards an end — an end which we today call death.' Finally: 'Every phase exists for the benefit of the whole and for the benefit of every other phase; if it is damaged, both the whole and every individual phase suffer.'

An excellent study of the human life-path, and one that is far more detailed and in my opinion more penetrating than that by Charlotte Bühler, has been written by another woman, *Martha Moers* of Bonn, and is entitled *Die Entwicklungsphasen des menschlichen Lebens* (The Development Phases in Human Life). In her foreword, Martha Moers states that it is her intention first and foremost to paint a picture of life as a *task*, a task which man has to complete with the help of his physical and soul-spiritual powers. The emphasis is laid on spiritual powers, for it is these that give life its true, deeper meaning, consistent with human dignity.

In the second place, Martha Moers tries to see the whole of human life as a more or less continuous development, viz. a development of the spiritual in man. This implies, at the same time, the requirement of self-education for the adult person.

The book gives a very complete survey of biological, psychic and spiritual factors in each phase of life. Here it is important that for the middle phase of adult life, the period between the beginning of the twenties and the beginning of the forties, the author introduces the concepts of *vital-psychological strivings, objective strivings* and *spiritual strivings*, and by painstaking observation and description produces a quite plausible account of how these three sorts of striving act dominantly in succession (become the *Wertmitte*, to use Guardini's term). For each phase of life she then goes on to describe its *general characteristics*, the *Werkschaffen*, or way in which a man approaches his tasks, its *social relations* and its *overall attitude to values*.

In Martha Moers's scheme of life there are six phases:

1. Childhood and youth, up to approximately 14 and 21 years of age
2. First adulthood and the twenties (21–28 years)
3. From approximately 28 to approximately 42 years
4. From approximately 42 to approximately 56 years
5. and 6. The two phases of old age (comparable with Rümke's *praesenium* and *senium*).

Her descriptions are characterized by tremendous thoroughness and, particularly where she discusses the relationships between work and values, she has some extremely original ideas. I have found neither of these two facets of the phases of life discussed elsewhere. They coincide very closely with my own experiences of adult education work.

In the coming pages I shall refer often to Martha Moers. Her work has remained relatively unknown, probably because it was published in an obscure university series. She is mentioned and quoted by no one, apart from Charlotte Bühler.

One's own view of the human life-path is indivisible from the image of man that has come to occupy the central position in one's own life. In addition, in my own case the person of *Rudolf Steiner* has had a strong influence. To Steiner, the concept of development is of crucial importance in his image of the world and of mankind. Starting from

Goethe's doctrine of metamorphosis for biological development and Schiller's theory of the threefold nature of human mental strivings, Steiner develops a completely new Goetheanism in which man is described in terms of body, soul and mind or spirit. The body, with predetermined laws of development, is created in a long period of development. Diametrically opposed to it is the mind, which, having become conscious in the human ego, is directed to the future and strives towards freedom. Between the two is the human soul or psyche — the stage upon which the two fields of force meet, and where man is man in the here and now.

Steiner, too, assumes ten seven-year periods in human development:

3 × seven years for physical and mental development
3 × seven years for true psychological development
3 × seven years for the development of the spirit.

Thus in 63 years man has passed through the stages of his development and then has a further seven-year period in order to consolidate them. At 70 he is then in a position to reap the fruits of his life and give them back to the community.

A word of warning is due here. None of the authors who describe seven or 14-year rhythms in the human life-path, not even Rudolf Steiner, believes that these rhythms manifest themselves on fixed dates in the calendar. Instead, they are milestones, averages, ideal distances around which individual development moves. Even so, they *are* yardsticks which may be used for the recognition of important deviations from the norm.

This might be a reason for looking for the causes of acceleration or retardation. In the years of childhood this is quite normal. A child who at seven years is not yet ready for school is suffering from some kind of disturbance in his development. The young person who passes through puberty when only nine, or not until 17, has usually already seen the doctor. The older a person becomes, the more capable he is of passing through accelerated or retarded phases of development without becoming a pathological case.

Steiner discusses three levels of mental development which he calls the sentient soul, the intellectual soul and the consciousness soul. Between the ages of 21 and 42 they may be discerned, one after the other, as the *Wertmitte* or dominating value-centre in human development. They correspond to the divisions described 30 years later by Martha Moers, who calls the same shift of dominant value-centres the vital-mental, objective and spiritual strivings. They are different names for the same phenomena.

I have now introduced the most important sources for our study of the phases of development in the human life-path. All have contributed towards making it possible for me to describe the human life-path itself in the coming chapters.

Chapter Two

The Course of Life

1. The Phases of Life

It is my intention to approach the human life-path from three angles:

(a) the biological
(b) the psychological
(c) the spiritual.

(a) The biological life-path
We have already seen that every living organism is chronotypically determined by its species.

If we estimate the duration of a human life to be 80 years, we may discern within that period the following three phases: a *period of growth*, during which constructive development outweighs decline; a *period of equilibrium* between development and decline; and a *period of involution*, a time of increasing decline.

The growth period up to about 20 years of age (a little earlier in girls, a little later in boys) is not a period of constant growth but comprises three phases in which increases in height and weight alternate. This process is described in greater detail in my book *Ontwikkelingsfasen van het kind* (The Development Phases of the Child), to which the reader

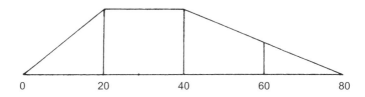

0   20   40   60   80

is referred for discussion of the problems associated with development in childhood.

Here, a short summary will suffice. The three phases of early development are

1. From birth until the first major increase in height and the second teething
2. From second teething to puberty
3. From puberty to adulthood.

Periods of *filling out* (becoming broader and heavier while growth in height is slow) alternate with phases of *stretching* (rapid growth in height during which the limbs, in particular, increase in length). The periods of stretching lie immediately before the second teething (at school age in Britain, just before school age on the Continent) and immediately before puberty. They are followed by periods of growth in breadth.

Nutrition has an important effect on the final *size* of the body, but *not* on the *rhythm* of the phases of development. Its influence is greatest during *critical phases*, which are different for different organs. For the brain, for example, the following points should be noted. During the first five months of life there is still considerable growth in the *number* of brain cells, and it is not until after this period that the increase is in the *size* of brain cells. Here, differentiation and growth succeed one another; of these, differentiation, the increase in the number of cells, is the more important. If during this phase the brain is subjected to malnutrition there will not subsequently be any possibility of repairing the damage, whereas later, when the cells themselves are increasing in size, it is possible to compensate for temporary malnutrition.

Thus it is extremely important to optimalize care during infancy, because it is precisely during this period that food shortages and disease have a permanent after-effect — a problem of crucial importance for the developing countries of the world.

The curve given above, which is highly schematic, shows a mean of growth, equilibrium and decline. Every organ system has its own chronotypical curve. Most people know that, for example, from about the age of 40 the lens of the eye becomes less flexible, accommodation falls off, and reading glasses often become necessary. For the ear the situation is different; from the age of 19 onwards the range of notes which the human ear can hear becomes compressed. In other words, as we grow older we hear less and less of the highest and lowest notes — or as one of my sons put it to me, 'You don't *need* a lot of expensive hi-fi equipment, father, you can't hear the top notes anyway.'

The range of hearing is quite easily determined, the result being called an audiogram. Mean audiograms for each age group have been established. Thus we may say that if someone aged, say, 35 has the audiogram of a 45-year-old, he has (at least as far as his hearing is concerned) aged prematurely. This may be sufficient reason for investigating whether perhaps other systems of organs may not also be declining prematurely. The period of involution is characterized by a decline in the elasticity of all body tissues. Not only the lens of the eye but also, for example, the entire lung system becomes less flexible, a fact which may be observed in the volume of air which one is capable of inhaling in a single breath, and which also becomes manifest in an increased period of breathlessness after running. That the walls of the blood vessels become stiff and even begin to degenerate is all too well known. In the coronary artery this diminished functioning is extremely dangerous, leading as it often does to a heart attack in which the walls of the artery gradually degenerate and the blood vessel silts up.

Some individuals deviate from the mean curve by premature ageing, others by staying 'young' for many years and being capable of vital performance until a late age. Even they, however, are likely to need reading glasses after the age of 40 and to tire more easily than in their youth.

The extent to which mental and spiritual functions run parallel with the phases of biological development will be discussed in a later chapter.

As we have already seen, Martha Moers approaches the phases of life from the angles of work performance, social relations, and the attitude to values. To a large degree this corresponds to the choice that I have made here, of biological, psychological and spiritual approaches. The next question we have to ask, then, is this: do the psychological and, later, the spiritual curves run parallel to the biological? Do they follow it or are they independent of it?

(b) The psychological life-path
In the first phase of growth until adulthood there is a clearly discernible line of development in the *psychological development* of thinking, feeling and willing which in its complex form and ever-changing content has been described in *Ontwikkelingsfasen van het kind* (The Development Phase of the Child).

Each of the three development phases in the main periods has a different theme as its leitmotiv.

In infancy the child is completely open to all impressions from outside and learns through imitation of its surroundings. The most important single thing that we can give the growing person for his path through life is a sense of assurance, trust and security — the feeling of being welcome in this world of people through which he receives love and warmth. Assurance and trust come from a rhythmic life and from consistency in the child's encounters; security comes from the warm love of his surroundings. In a word, the child must be given a basic sense that *the world is good*. The phase after the first stretching and the second teething, i.e. the schoolchild phase, is characterized by greatly increased seclusion; the child turns more towards himself, and explores the qualities of his own mind in thinking, feeling and willing. The child does this with the power of fantasy. In effect he now lives in his own garden surrounded by a high wall; inside it the child builds a world of his own in which he can do everything that he cannot yet do in the real world outside.

This childish fantasy lays the foundations for creativity in the social life and career of later years. An individual who has been unable for whatever reason to fantasize and daydream during this phase will later sense a lack of spontaneity and versatility in interpersonal relations. Intellectualist education stifles fantasy and breeds people who later in life become lonely and are continually confronted with their inability to make real contact with other people. The fact that this weakness of contact has assumed almost epidemic proportions is hardly surprising in view of our system of primary education. Artistically minded teaching, creative play and story-telling by parents all exercise the mobility of the mental faculties and nurture originality and spontaneity.

During the second phase the child must be convinced that the world is full of joy and full of beauty. Beauty in this context has a different meaning for the child than for the adult who is incapable of appreciating the beauty of a single beetle or leaf or pebble.

The third phase (puberty and adolescence) provides the great breakthrough to reality. As early as the pre-pubertal stage the protective child-world to which I have referred is broken, and the young person finds himself faced with a reality that is often unfriendly. The results of this shattering of the child's fantasy world include loneliness in puberty, the sense of being understood by no one, and a tendency towards hero-worship. In adolescence (which I take to begin at 16 to 17) there follows the task of finding an attitude (albeit a temporary one) to the world.

Here, then, the child moves into the search, described in *Ontwikkelingsfasen van het kind* (The Development Phases of the Child), for a *Weltanschauung*, an ideology or picture of the world, the religious striving and the political striving which at this age has a religious character, and finally the choice of final education and career (for those who are in a position to complete their natural development). In effect we have here the awakening of the search for truth: what is 'the world' really like?

Plato already saw that goodness, beauty and truth were the foundations of humanity. In youth they must be given the chance to unfold in order later to grow into morality, creativity and wisdom. This development depends not on external prosperity but on inner 'fullness'.

As long ago as 1945 writers were putting forward the idea that it was a crime to force children into a career or factory work at the age of 14 or 15. In such a situation they are unable to complete the third phase of their growth towards adulthood. The fact that at present formative, so-called participation education is being given to this very large group is only a first step. Every human being has the right to general formative education until his eighteenth year, so that later he can and may make his contribution to society as a complete person.

In *Ontwikkelingsfasen van het kind* (The Development Phases of the Child) I drew attention to the close correlation between physical and mental development. In the early years it is more or less absolute. The slightest stomach disorder or impending illness is first noticeable in the child's behaviour — he becomes listless and irritable. After puberty the child's psychological development makes a clear break from total dependence on biological events, even though the interdependence is still greater than in later years.

And what happens then? In answering this question we have arrived at the central point of this book: the vital-mental drive follows the biological life-path quite closely, whereas the spiritual-mental functions divorce themselves increasingly from it and can even be at their zenith when the biological functions have already declined to a severe degree. It is for this reason that it is not possible to draw one clear chronotypical line of development for psychological development. In the first 20-odd years biological and psychological functions run largely parallel, after which they influence one another *mutually* to a very high degree (the psychosomatic oneness of man is especially clearly present in the middle phase of life). But in the course of the forties there comes the time when the vital-mental functions begin to diminish. The vital drive towards an active life, towards getting to grips with the world, declines. It becomes increasingly difficult to produce the same performance at work. We begin to feel threatened by the following generation, which still has the vitality which we ourselves are now losing, and so on. This process will have to be described in greater detail. Only when the spiritual-mental functions are awakened in the middle phase of life can they take over the task of the declining vital-mental functions.

Thus in the course of the forties we see two new types of further development (with every shade of degree between the two extremes): *either* our experience of our own value is measured against the external performance which we have hitherto been able to produce, in which case we arrive at a crisis, *or* we experience a sense of our own worth in the help we can give others. A new phase in our social life can begin, in which accumulated experience can be dispensed to those around us. As regards the work situation this phase may be characterized as that in which we gradually begin to stand back from our work and see it in a wider social context. For those in management this means a transition from managing things by organizing everything oneself to managing things by forming policy in the execution of which *others* can develop their powers.

This last phase after the beginning of the forties can therefore be described as the social or policy phase. But bear in mind that this is a possibility, not a certainty! Although it is naturally far from ideal to try and show these complex and qualitatively so different processes in one diagram, we shall see that the diagram on the following page nevertheless does tell us something.

(c) The spiritual life-path
The spiritual development of man expresses itself initially in the ego-consciousness which arises in the toddler phase, in the ego-experience of the schoolchild phase, and in the drive towards ego-realization in adolescence. In the middle phase of life ego-consciousness, ego-experience and ego-realization can go through a further development which will be described later. It becomes visible from the outside in the spiritual-mental strivings of a person in the finding, experiencing and application of norms in interpersonal relations, in work performance and attitudes to work, and in the faculty of finding an area of interest outside the necessity of the situation. In other words, the faculty of

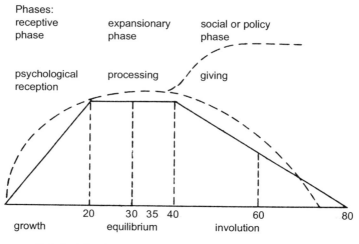

raising oneself *above* the stimulus-response situation which still characterizes the vital-mental drive.

The individual who has already found an interest in art, science, nature or social work in the middle phase of his life will pass the great divide in his or her life-path after the age of 40 almost without noticing it, and will be able to live increasingly from a spiritual source. On the other hand, the person who in his middle phase has done nothing else but chase personal success, pushing aside everything that might interfere with his career, or who has allowed his life to be governed exclusively by his work and by other external circumstances, will find himself after the age of 40 in an existential crisis, and by the time he is 55 will have become a tragic figure, everlastingly appealing to the good old days and finding nothing but threats in all that is new.

The *biological* rhythms in development have their most profound effect in the period *before* adulthood; *psychological* development manifests itself in its own logic most clearly during the middle phase; *spiritual* development is characteristic of the final phase of life.

2. Adolescence

'The main business of the adolescent is to stop being one.'
(Cole and Hall, *The Psychology of Adolescence*).
'To be human is to live in each phase of life.'
(Guardini, *Die Lebensalter* [The Periods of Life])

The preliminary phase: adolescence (from 16–17 to 21–24).

In the crisis of the years of maturation, in puberty, the personality of the individual starts to become apparent. This 'wakening' of the personality is continued during adolescence, and constitutes the axis around which everything turns. At least, if it does not, the individual remains dependent upon his environment, or stubbornly maintains an adolescent attitude of rebellion towards whatever he sees as authority.

The crucial questions are therefore: Who am I? What do I want? What am I capable of?

It is precisely because these crucial questions have yet to be answered that it now becomes clear what Rümke means when he describes the characteristics of adolescence as a sense of impermanence, the lack of a fixed base or destination, and disillusion with regard to the ideas of puberty.

The tasks of the individual at this stage in his life therefore include 'the unification of sensual (biological) *sexuality* and *psychological eroticism*'. We become aware of the former during puberty, whereas the latter must awaken in adolescence so that in the next phase we can begin to experience the initial blossoming of love for the personality of another human being.

Künkel, too, discusses in detail the significance of psychological eroticism for the years of adolescence. He writes: '*Die Seele erglüht im Du − die Welt des Du, der sich dem Eros erchliesst,*' and '*Die Welt erglüht, sobald die Seele erglüht.*'* He thereby refers to the fact that in this phase of life the individual is living *from the inside outwards* to a very high degree. For the person in love the whole world looks different. Life *as it is experienced* is determined by the *experience* of the realities of the world, not by the objective significance of those realities. In this connection Künkel also says '*das Schicksal kommt von Innen*' −our fate comes from within. Through eroticism we see reality anew, and it is only now that the personal choice of a path through life becomes possible. So that the danger of adolescence is that sexuality may persist unaccompanied by the awakening of eroticism.

The concept of eroticism that I am using here is the same as what in the Middle Ages used to be called courtly or

---

* 'The Soul glows in the you−the world of you which opens itself to Eros.' −'The world glows as soon as the Soul glows.'

romantic love. By the end of the age of chivalry love had become a cultural factor. The minnesingers sang of the pure romantic attachment between man and woman. Love was the reverence of a man for the feminine ideal and of a woman for the masculine ideal. When the knight in battle or at a tournament fought for the name of his lady there was no hint of sexuality in the relationship between them. Love was practised as an art, just as music is an art; the game element was paramount, and love, like every game, was played according to predetermined rules.

Becoming aware of love was an overwhelming experience for a young man or woman, but it was not yet a personal matter. Only spiritual love, born of meeting and recognizing the *other ego*, gave the inner security which led to faithfulness to the individuality of the partner. In Wolfram von Eschenbach's *Parzival*, Parzival and Gawain perform many chivalrous deeds despite their unshaken love-relationships with Kondwiramur and Orgeluse respectively.

Eroticism is a stage in the development of the soul, but not yet of the spirit.

I shall go into the difference between biological sex, psychological eroticism and spiritual love in greater detail in the chapter on marriage. Here this path of development of the psyche becomes reality. 'The great human drama is only just beginning.'

Guardini describes adolescence as the continuation of the crisis of the years of puberty. It begins with the awakening of the person—the experience of 'consciously wanting to be someone distinct from everyone else'.

The situation is one in which the lifting power of vitality underlines and reinforces development. Bound up with a still absent experience of the tough resistance of reality, a lack of a sense of reality arises which creates the unconditionality of every judgement and causes every compromise to be rejected. Guardini calls this 'the infinity of the still untried beginning'. True ideas and the appropriate attitude should be capable of altering reality. There is a tendency towards a short-circuiting of judgement and action, 'all the more violent according as the personal ego is still *unsure* of itself'.

The grand idea, the protest against injustice, is over-estimated in its effect. What is still lacking is the 'fundamental attitude of patience' with regard to reality, with its concomitant factors of mediocrity and commonplaceness. But this same inexperience with the resistances of reality can also give rise to the courage necessary for a decision about life which will then need decades to be put into effect. Even the mere choice of a career is always a daring venture. Part of the way in which Guardini orders his problems when referring to the phases of life is his continuous search for that *configuration of values* which controls and guides the phase of life by making choices in a particular direction. It is this configuration, as we have already seen, that he calls the 'dominant value-centre', the *Wertmitte*.

For adolescence this configuration of values is 'taking oneself upon oneself', that is, learning to accept oneself and thereby being able to answer questions for oneself (and making choices and decisions). This is the same as being able to start bearing one's own, individual, responsibility. But on the path which leads to this the necessary experience must be gained: 'everyone has to commit his own follies'. The only condition is that one be willing to learn from them.

Guardini points out with some emphasis that each phase of life has its *own* task in the development of the individual, and quotes Goethe: 'We travel not only to arrive but to live while travelling.' These words are of great importance in considering the significance of adolescence. They are in flagrant opposition to the first of the two mottoes quoted at the beginning of this chapter—a motto, then, which comes from a different school of thought on the subject of development. Cole and Hall's book *The Psychology of Adolescence* gives a virtually complete survey of everything there is to know about adolescence from the standpoint of behaviourism and empiricism. As such it is a useful handbook, starting as it does from the basic premise that 'in order to pass from childhood to adulthood an adolescent *must solve* a number of problems'.

Adolescence is here seen as a *transit phase* in which problems have to be solved before the individual can pass from being a child to the adulthood which he desires so much to achieve. There are nine of these problems: (1) general emotional maturity; (2) the bringing about of heterosexual interest; (3) general social maturity; (4) emancipation from the parental home; (5) intellectual maturity; (6) choice of a career; (7) learning to use leisure; (8) the construction of a psychology of life, culminating in behaviour based on conscience and a sense of duty; (9) identification, or perception, of one's self.

It is therefore a time of hard work at highly disparate tasks, resulting in behaviour such that one may be termed adult — adulthood being apparently the purpose of the adolescent phase. In other words, to summarize: the main business of the adolescent is to stop being one.

The overall after-taste left by this extremely comprehensive and excellent book is: what a wretched time adolescence is — eat your way through the rice-pudding mountain of the nine tasks as quickly as possible to get into the promised paradise of true adulthood, real life!

But adolescence is a *genuine phase of life*, with a *style of its own*, with joys and sorrows which signify an essential quality in the totality of life. This quality is Guardini's *Wertmitte* — having the courage of one's convictions and thereby maintaining one's task of inner freedom. For this a healthy development of the ego is necessary. In *Ontwikkelingsfasen van het kind* (The Development Phases of the Child) I distinguish between three steps in this ego-development: *ego-consciousness*, beginning at about the third birthday; *ego-experience*, beginning in the primary school period and breaking through into pre-puberty; and *ego-realization* in adolescence. At the same time we must bear in mind that every new aspect of development gives the previous aspects new content. Through puberty and beginning adolescence the childish ego-consciousness acquires a new quality. In puberty the closed world of the child had already been broken open and the reality of the world made visible.

The question is now: Where do *I* stand in the world? What is this world really *like*? What forces are at play in it? What is the balance of power? In other words, what do I mean *in* the world?

The experience of the ego, too, ties up with this. The ego-experience nuance of pre-puberty leads the individual to turn sharply inwards to himself and his own experiences. In asking himself what he means in the world the child is turning his attention to the outside again, though still, for the time being, in uncertainty. The question now becomes a broader one: What can I believe in? Where do I aim my ideals? Is there something higher by which I may raise myself up, which can serve as my lodestar?

The ego-realization places the ego in the social reality with contemporaries and older people. (At this moment younger people hardly play any part, unless as a refuge from his contemporaries.) And alongside this new regulation of social problems the choice of further education and a career (for those who can still choose and have not already been 'thrown in at the deep end') now occupies a central position.

The choice of career demands considerable self-knowledge *and* knowledge of the world, for the reality of the professions and trades has become obscure to those outside them, while many training opportunities fail to be sufficiently publicized. The result is that this vital choice is made during adolescence more or less at random. The fact that so many students fail examinations, give up their studies or change courses before finishing their degrees illustrates the perils of a system that requires school pupils to determine the paths of their future educational and professional careers at some time between the ages of 15 and 18. Conversations with school-leavers reveal that many of them feel that they have landed themselves in a net when they realize how much their freedom of choice in the matter of a career has been limited by their choice of subjects at school — a choice often made on the basis of class-marks during the years of puberty!

For those who already find themselves in employment or otherwise pledged to a particular trade or profession at the age of 15 or 16, the foregoing applies to an even more serious degree. Luckily it is nowadays possible to change one's job by means of all sorts of retraining courses and training courses organized within the firm. That this is the rule rather than the exception is illustrated by the fact that only a very small proportion of those who take a vocational course at the age of 14 or 15 are still working in the same field after ten years.

In the years of adolescence everything still has a certain absoluteness, and yet at the same time a certain quality of temporariness — a remarkable and self-contradictory situation, but one which the adolescent himself does not find in any way disturbing. Judgements and feelings are absolute — for the moment! All choices are 'provisional — absolute'.

University courses and other forms of education unnaturally prolong the adolescence situation until far into the twenties, and thus disturb the healthy development of the first adulthood, which depends partly on the individual having his own responsibilities. The fact that students today demand a share in the responsibility for their own study situation is a healthy reaction to a dependence which has gone on for too long. When such demands begin to acquire an absolutist and dogmatic character, that is in turn a symptom of prolonged adolescence.

The most important problem facing the adolescent, as stated earlier, is finding his own relationship to the social reality of the culture and time in which he lives. But what *is* this social reality? How does it come about? The answer can only be: it is made by people.

Schiller's theory of the three principles operating in social life may give us some guidance here. In what he calls the *Formtrieb*, the 'form drive', man is unfree, tied to spiritual laws and logic and to phrase, convention and routine. In the *Stofftrieb*, the 'material drive', he is subject to the laws of nature and physical existence—again, he is unfree. In everyday life among other people he can create his own free world between the laws of the spirit and the laws of nature.

Freedom within this everyday world, however, is constantly threatened by the ancient ethic of 'thou shalt and thou shalt not', and by the dogmas of the 'scientifically justifiable' images of man and the world. At the same time, it is threatened by the harsh reality of physical existence with the need to earn money in order to live or else be dependent on others.

Between form and matter what Schiller calls the *Spieltrieb*, the 'play drive', can develop. He characterizes this as man's highest creative faculty. The margin of freedom which is the lifesaver for the adolescent may be found between mind and matter. What is important is that despite limitations imposed by physical circumstances and by cultural taboos and the accepted norms of the concrete social situation he *makes* something that is totally and absolutely *personal*. The freedom of meeting with people, nature and culture then suddenly emerges as being too great. It is part of everybody's liberty that he should be able, with or without money, to 'see' nature or to swagger his way through it, to 'meet' his fellow being or to walk past him.

This freedom within the situation must be discovered and practised during adolescence. Often we are helped by an unusual situation to lift a meeting out of the common rut.

A person who starts drawing in spite of his belief that he cannot draw suddenly sees the world anew and in an unknown light. The man who practises dramatic expression in a group suddenly sees himself and others in their unfreedom of movement *and* in the liberating leap out of convention. Many forms of group therapy and of therapy based on artistic expression are founded on the provision of an opportunity of developing a bit of *Spieltrieb* and hence an inner equilibrium.

For the place which the adolescent intends to take in social life it is of great importance that he should be able at an early stage to experience a measure of edifying exercise in creative and social skills, so that with the new eyes which this new ability gives him he can see for himself something of the difficult situation facing him in the welfare state.

Every culture passes on both benefits and problems to the following generations. In more spiritually inclined cultures, such as that of Ancient India, all energy and all questions were directed at spiritual problems. And he who serves the spirit is rewarded by the spirit with rich fruits. He who, as for example in western society, devotes all his zeal and perseverance to material things will acquire material things in abundance—in such abundance, indeed, that they will bring about his downfall. We are already far gone in our preoccupation with the latter. The adolescent who sees this crazy race with new, unprejudiced eyes seeks a contrary force in the other pole.

With all this it is difficult for the adolescent of today to find a creative attitude which he may call his own. Social structures have all undergone enlargement of dimension, and that, in the social field, leads to increased mental and spiritual loneliness and alienation.

Blauner has described this problem excellently as being characterized by alienation, increased isolation, senseless-ness, and powerlessness. He has also established that all these things are least in evidence where the individual is closely involved with his work and his employer (a situation which may equally well exist in an office environment), that they are most clearly to be seen in the mechanical labour of large groups, and that they are again less obvious where small groups have clearly defined responsibilities and a certain measure of freedom of action in their work.

The conclusions to be drawn from this kind of research also apply to the present situation in our universities. Whereas in the past small groups of students worked closely with a professor, the student who nowadays wishes to attend a lecture has to fight his way through a sea of his fellows in order to hear a distant figure on a stage tell a story. However important they may be for education, and however heroic attempts to make them work may be, with the numbers of students now attending European universities seminars cannot compensate for the imbalance in the student-teacher ratio. That is only possible in later years, when up to half the newcomers have 'evaporated', as a vice-chancellor put it to me recently.

The 'evaporation' which is the lot of many thousands of young people is coupled in the individual with feelings of despair and insufficiency, and can leave a permanent scar on a person's life. In my experience as a student psychiatrist I have seen the 'other side' of the evaporation process. It would be a very good thing if adolescents were better prepared for this frustrating situation when they embarked upon their course of study.

The reverse of the position of a student is that of young factory workers, both skilled and unskilled. In the middle of puberty this very large section of the community is suddenly shifted from the schoolroom onto the shop floor. At once they are in a society of adults, with adult working hours and adult mores. They are deprived of their adolescence, and self-discovery takes place in a single sudden shock at a moment when the ego is not yet mature enough to control the process. Although material independence here becomes a fact at a very early stage in the individual's life, and, since he has little else, is endowed with considerable and exaggerated importance, there is also a large degree of spiritual constraint in the formation of a picture of the world and the judgement of cultural and social situations.

Day-release and other adult education and participant education connected with vocational training is a step in the right direction but remains in essence a palliative. I repeat: *every human being has a right to general education until his eighteenth year*. That such education need not cover the same ground for everyone, not even for people in the same 'stream', but that it should be flexible in order to meet the needs and accommodate the capabilities of each individual, goes almost without saying.

I cannot close this chapter without saying something about the 'adolescent revolution' which has been front-page news almost continuously since 1968. To begin with, we may make a couple of observations. First, the 'struggle for democratization' is generally led by people whose adolescence lies behind them but who show clear signs of the character structures of a disturbed or insufficiently developed process of adolescence. This results in the persistence of development situations which ought already to have been overcome—fanatical idealism and a lack of consideration for the individual's fellow beings, and a concomitant simplification of complex problems and a 'scapegoat mentality'. The real solutions lie not in any 'violent democracy' but in learning to be creative in concrete human situations. The structural aspect of the society in which we live can only be approached fruitfully when maturity in social relations has been brought about. That the creation of such a climate is a time-consuming and laborious task with ever-changing and surprising new starting-points will become clear in the following chapters. It remains a fact of life that there are many different forms of maturity, in the biography of the individual human being as elsewhere. A just society has a duty to offer equal chances for survival to all of them.

To sum up, we may say that the central problem of adolescence is: *Who am I? What do I want? What am I capable of?* The individual who has failed to ask these questions in this phase of life—even if only by realizing that he suffers from not knowing the answers—has failed to lay the foundations for the awakening of his psychological being, so that he runs the risk in the important middle phase of life of finding himself stuck at the passionately vital stage, an eternal adolescent who in his appreciation of values remains dependent on what the world thinks of him, or who, on account of his own insecurity, continues to kick against the world.

This description of adolescence is what may be termed ideal-typical. For some readers it may make an old-fashioned impression—adolescents may have been like that 50 years ago, but things have changed. In the meantime an evolution has taken place. We have been liberated from many taboos. The sexual element is familiar territory to every adolescent, and 'eroticism', as described here, a product of a bourgeois morality which has since been overcome.

Those in late adolescence and young adults in their twenties are generally considered to have become more aware of things; ideas which assume the happily married couple to be in their twenties and to have small children crawling about their feet are ideas of at least 30 years ago. In their place, we have free relationships and couples living together with generally no thought yet of having children.

All this is seen as something quite new. But if we examine such problems with a rather greater historical awareness, we find that when we go back more than a century or so sexuality was the same subject for open discussion as it has now been rediscovered to be, while sexual relations in adolescence, though publicly forbidden, were a well-regulated institution, particularly in country districts.

In fact there was only one century of 'Victorian' bourgeois morality, with its hypocrisy and double standards, by which anything went as long as it did so in private. But even this dual morality (in which, of course, men could do what they liked, while women could do nothing) had its code. Relationships were expected to be serious and to mean rather more than the satisfying of animal drives with whoever happened to be handy.

The hypocrisy of the bourgeois classes has now been broken down again. Young people are allowed to live together — though they are still supposed to be serious about it to some extent. That is, eroticism now plays a role alongside sex. Even so, this is true only for a small part of the population of Europe: for the bourgeois classes themselves. For country folk and for young working people in the towns and cities nothing has changed; for them, there always was a large measure of freedom, governed by the code that when a girl became pregnant the boy was not allowed to get ideas about not marrying her — an understandable attitude at a time of primitive contraception methods.

In about 1925, when I was a student, I went to stay with a cousin who was a doctor in a country area. One Sunday afternoon he was called to the front door. Coming back inside for a moment, he invited me, with a broad grin on his face, to go outside with him to enjoy the fun. It was a band of young people who had come, as was the custom in those parts, to announce the forthcoming marriage of two of their number. 'They don't have to' was the repeated cry — and *that* meant that it was to be an unusually special and respectable marriage!

Over the years I have had a great deal to do with young factory workers, and at a time when bourgeois (and academic) young people still lived under 'Victorian' rule I came across the same blind acceptance of the standards of old. There was a fixed pattern of surveying the market, courtship and marriage. But here too the game of attraction and rejection is present just as much as it is in the romantic era. One only has to listen to the girls at work on the conveyor belt. Their hands flick to and fro automatically, and so do exchanges like: 'Did you see Gerry yesterday? I'll swear he was winking at Carol. You'd better look out.'

The laws which govern human development lie deeper than any phenomenon of fashion, and many a modern freedom is no more than the re-emergence of a freedom that existed centuries ago. And that freedom covered the development of the body, spirit and soul — despite the latest fashion of only letting the first of these three reach the forefront.

3. Early Adulthood — the Twenties

At 21 the individual has reached adulthood and is responsible for his own actions. This long-standing legal position is the concrete result of a judgement about responsibility which is itself founded in a pre-scientific knowledge. And although the moment is not really a moment at all, but a process of transition and subject to individual and political influences, it is nevertheless well chosen as a fixation point, both biologically and psychologically.

In dividing life into phases we run up against a problem: it is not possible to determine a *moment* of transition from one phase to the next. As has been remarked elsewhere, it is like the change from day into night. Adolescence slides gradually into adulthood until the characteristics of the latter predominate.

Inwardly, the beginning of adulthood is experienced in a positive sense; after the doubts and transience of adolescence the individual begins to be able to see something of the future. There is a powerful vital drive towards expansion in many fields. The foundation of the person's own living unit and the beginning of a career are the two most important aspects for the man. For the woman, it is the acquisition of her responsibility for shaping an environment which is usually most important. Where this moment is postponed because of external circumstances, it is felt inwardly to be a deprivation, and is repressed. But in each instance creativity of no mean proportions has to be developed.

Seeking and finding a partner, finding and furnishing somewhere to live, and the initial phases of a career are all clear external manifestations of an inner mental structure. Two individuals now have to build up their own life-style. How do we relate to each other? How do we eat? How do we give shape to our evenings? Are we to make something of our moments together—breakfast, homecoming? Are we *really* going to talk to each other? Are we going to react to each other, or is there going to be nothing but a series of brief observations without mutual interest in what is going on inside our partners' minds? How is the house going to be furnished and decorated? Will it express something personal? Is it to be a furniture showroom or a sort of junk-room for whatever happens to find its way into the home?

All this applies not only to the actual concrete surroundings of a life together but also to the marriage itself. Anyone who has experience of taking on staff will know that a home visit can reveal more about a person and his background than a dry conversation at the office. The new life-style is the creation of a piece of culture, the establishment of an environment, because it is the environment itself which will shape the new generation. This is also true of the manner of interpersonal relations. The baby crawling around between the table-legs does not yet comprehend the content of the parents' action towards each other. But the fact that the father can say something and that the mother can reply, 'Yes, that's what *you* say, but I see it differently,' without the one attacking and morally judging the other, and so on—in short, the shape of the discussion—and the mutual respect and the freedom which each gives the other, all these are part of the child's experience, and even at this early stage they are shaping the child's attitude to life long before he has managed to grasp their content.

Differentiation in language usage, too, is a formative influence on the young child. The building up of this living-space, physically and mentally, demands much energy and interest, but also provides a great deal of satisfaction. An equally creative effort in the social sphere is involved in the individual's establishing himself or herself in a job. At whatever level a person starts, he is always confronted with the necessity of gaining the appreciation of his superiors and colleagues. For without that, the individual is not living psychologically a 'livable' 'soul-space'.

One's first job is only the stirrup by means of which one climbs into the saddle—it then becomes necessary for one to prove oneself in the field. During the twenties the individual's emotional life is still violent and unstable. When Goethe was 27 he looked back on the past phase of his life and characterized it with the immortal words: '*Himmelhoch jauchzend—zum Tode betrübt.*' ('Exulting to the heavens, distressed unto death.')

The individual's sense of his own worth is still very much dependent on how the world reacts to his or her (expansionary) actions and work. If his superiors have praised his work, the world is full of sunshine, and celebrations are in order at home. After a reprimand or the failure of a piece of work, the whole world is a nasty and gloomy place.

The young adult needs to test his ability under many different circumstances in order so to discover himself. In olden days this was the journeyman phase, when one moved from master to master, each time learning something new in different circumstances. Modern working life offers few opportunities for this unless, contrary to the general tendency, one takes the initiative oneself.

The worst thing that can happen to a person during these years is that he has to do the same work for ten years on end without learning anything from his work. The stronger characters escape from this trap by starting their own careers anew, and staying in each job until they have learnt all they need or all there is to learn. However the majority, following a period of rebelliousness, resign themselves to their fate, having learnt for the rest of their lives not to take initiative. Increasing dependence on external security and social provisions is a natural reaction.

During the twenties, and especially in the second half of the twenties, the individual's inner, psychological life takes on its first personal shape. This is the shape which Rudolf Steiner calls the 'sentient soul' and Martha Moers the 'vital-mental strivings'. Following Grossart, she characterizes these by saying that it is not until now that the individual's mind becomes a closed unity capable of being experienced as such: 'These, the vital-mental strivings, cannot be explained as a simple intensifying (*Steigerung*) or sublimation of the biological drives, but represent something that is specifically new, a leap forward in mental development that far transcends what is biologically logical and hence also the sphere of drives and instincts.

'Initially these powers are still very much directed at themselves, and are experienced above all in feelings, but they are already leading to the need to occupy oneself with spiritual problems and to see oneself in a development which spans the entire arc of life.'

Personally, I should put it like this. Within the individual there emerges an inner world in which the drives stemming from the body constitute only one of the parameters. Other parameters of equivalent value include a knowledge of one's own life as a task and as an entity — not merely a knowledge, but also a direct experience of beginning and end, of point and pointlessness, of voluntarily chosen responsibility towards people and social institutions.

The entire middle phase of life, from early adulthood until the beginning of the forties, is the phase in which a *rich inner life* develops with its many facets and the concomitant externally-oriented objectives.

The first phase, that of the 'sentient soul' and the 'vital-mental strivings', is thus also the phase in which a powerful emotional life emerges and endows the individual with his first provisional shape. That this feeling of 'being in the process of becoming' a person in one's own right is at first still tentative is understandable, and is expressed in the flexibility of feelings and in the trying-out of one's own capacities in private interpersonal relations and in life in the work environment.

Martha Moers believes that the development of the woman during these years follows a slightly different course — primarily because the *Nachreife* (the transitional phase from adolescence to adulthood) has already ended by the age of 21, whereas in the man it may continue until the age of about 24. 'As regards maturity of personality, the woman is therefore, for the moment, the man's superior.' At the same time the nature of women drives the individual woman more towards the *seelische Liebe*, spiritual love. In the woman, sexuality has always been permeated with aspects connected with motherhood, including spiritual motherliness, even in less developed personalities.

This means that at the beginning of her adulthood the woman is faced with a dual task which often leads to an inner conflict. She has to put all her strength into the continuation of the human race, for which she has to bear the full burden. On the other hand modern life requires her intensive participation in the male-organized career work of public life. The woman is involved in this conflict as early as adolescence, and thereafter to an increasing degree. If the girl marries, she can devote herself to her specifically female role. These tasks are so important for the development of the woman because they promote the reinforcement of the 'mental-spiritual strivings'.

Early adulthood is also the phase of life in which the development from sex to love by way of eroticism is determined for the rest of the individual's life. The child becomes a person in the love of his parents, he then experiences the awakening of eroticism in the form of the play element in his growing up, and discovers sexuality during the period of biological maturation, in the preliminary stages of puberty. (Here I am not in agreement with the view of the psychoanalytical school that the drives in the emotional life of childhood must be regarded as sexuality. In my opinion this is a misuse of the concept, which has diverted attention from the development from sex to love via eroticism.) Depending on individual and cultural circumstances, this first meeting with sexuality may be a shock, an overwhelming experience, or no more than an incident. In adolescence the child is given the opportunity of rediscovering eroticism, this time in relation to the opposite sex.

Eroticism is the element of the soul in which attraction and repulsion, hope and disappointment, question and answer fly back and forth. Eroticism can develop separately from biological sexuality in friendship and respect; eroticism is the great inspiration of the arts, particularly poetry and music. It evolves into love when the soul opens itself to another person, when the one can experience the other within himself in such a way that the other knows that he has been recognized in the lover. This complex of problems is an important factor in the early twenties.

The choice of partner may be purely a question of biological sex, in which case it is not likely to be of any great durability. On the other hand, it may begin on a sexual basis and grow into an intimate play of small surprises and initiatives meaning more for the soul than for the body, and may then progress to become love for the spiritual make-up of the partner, who only then knows that he or she has really been recognized and hence appealed to and spurred on in the development of a spiritual humanity.

It is in this initial stage that the seeds are sown for a possible later development in the marriage relationship. That, too, demands a considerably expansionary character directed towards inner development. If that development fails to take place now it will be particularly difficult during the thirties, as we shall see later, so that in the crisis of the forties the individual is left empty-handed.

Towards the age of 28 (an age which is mentioned by virtually all researchers in this field) the waves of emotion become less strong, the intellectual approach begins to count more heavily, and distance from events increases. After this we see the first backward glance, a clearly defined sense of the final break from youth as a whole, the pre-monition and prescience of a phase in which quite different tasks impress themselves while the spontaneity of emotional development shifts to the background. In many biographies and discussions we find that 'youth has passed — now begins the serious business of living'.

4. The Organizational Phase

'Um das achtundzwanzigste Jahr herum muss der Mensch erleben, dass die jugendliche Form des Eros in ihm erstirbt.' (Künkel, Die Lebensalter [The Periods of Life]*

The next phase, beginning towards the end of the twenties and lasting until the mid-thirties, is of quite a different

---

* 'About his twenty-eighth year man must experience that the youthful form of Eros within himself dies away.'

character from the previous one. 'Youth' is now past, the serious business of living has finally begun. This fact becomes evident in many ways. The changes of job in previous years now cease. Now the challenge is to push in order to make a firm bond with one's work, and to find within it either a means of rising towards or to the top, or at least to some broadening of responsibility. The individual's attitude is now more intellectual; the expansionary drive is still there and is still carried along by considerable vitality, but now it is the intellectual aspect that is beginning to predominate. By about 30 the individual has carried out his first evaluation of himself; he knows what he is capable of, where his problems lie, and what will probably be unachievable. The twenties were a fertile period of testing his own aspirations; now he must work out a campaign plan.

Rudolf Steiner calls this the development of the 'intellectual soul', Martha Moers uses the term 'objective strivings' — again, we have two ways of expressing the same thing.

From the career point of view, we may call this phase *the organizational phase*, because during it we have a tendency to solve problems by means of organization. Surveying a field, analysing the factors involved, taking logical decisions based on observed and researched facts and prognoses — this is the attitude which now comes to the forefront. At the same time, especially for men, there is an increasing need to couple organizational ability with a position of power. As early as the 1920s Künkel wrote: '*Der Ausdruck des ersten Mannesalters ist der Befehl. Kurz, knapp, scharf umrissen, rücksichtslos muss alles sein. Zwischen Befehl und Gehorsam, im nüchternen Dienst an einem organisatorischen Werk, findet der Mensch zwischen 30 und 40 seine Erfüllung.*' (Early manhood is expressed in orders. Everything must be brief, concise, sharply delineated, ruthless. Between orders and obedience, in sober service of a work of organization, man finds fulfilment between the ages of 30 and 40.) And though this way of putting it may sound terribly German, if we look about us, especially at the management attitudes that have come across from America, we see that the veracity of Künkel's statement is confirmed in the life of industry and commerce. The main thing is to have 'placed' oneself before one's fortieth birthday. For the commonly held view is that anyone who has not become clearly visible by that time will be passed for further promotion.

At 35, the man is at the zenith of his capacity for work, certainly in quantitative terms. Within his characterological structure he has built up considerable self-assurance. Life lies in his pocket. He knows what he can and will achieve, and is striving towards that goal with logical persistence. He believes that all problems (including personal ones) can be solved through logical organization. This is the phase of life in which, within his own personality structure, he is most materialistic.

But what about the woman? She too goes through an intellectual phase. For her the twenty-eighth/twenty-ninth year is an even greater transition and farewell to past things than it is for the man. In her thirties she too is required to make a relatively large contribution in the organizational sphere. Her children are beginning to grow up and go to various different schools which have different hours. To get each child out of the house in good time, equipped with everything he needs both materially and psychologically, and then to have the house in order before the first child comes home for lunch (assuming, of course, that they don't all have lunch at school), and *then* be able to provide each child with whatever he needs, and *then* to be attractive and good company in the evening — all this demands just as much organizational ability as does the running of a company by the man.

In the biography of very many of the people I have been able to talk to, both patients and people in good health and employment, the beginning of the thirties is inwardly the most peaceful period of their lives, relatively speaking. By that I mean that much may be happening on the surface, but that their inner equilibrium and sense of security are at a peak.

The initial passion of being in love has now passed. As we have already seen, other sources have to be tapped in advance if the marriage is not to dry out into a sober, businesslike relationship in which each partner has his duties and in which sexual life becomes a routine without there being much to experience in it. Only a mutual spiritual bond can guide the marriage to a later, new phase.

Thirty-five — life's major achievement! Faust is 35 when he makes his pact with Mephisto, because he feels that he has arrived at a dead end. Dante embarks upon his great journey because he feels as though he is in a dark forest from which no path can lead him into the open. In fact, both these examples are examples of experience of a later period, an *Ahnung* or premonition of other aspects of life than the sober and objective. In my experience such 'premonitions' in our own times occur only towards the end of the thirties or in the early forties. For the moment the world is there to be tackled and changed. The individual has made his choice and is ready to accept the consequences of his choice.

The self-image of the person now becomes more clearly defined, more clearly visible. The individual begins to have faith in himself, and believes that life will now continue along the same lines. The danger of a hardening of attitudes and of egotism is now particularly great. The individual often buries himself in his work and lays the foundations for his own social isolation. He makes no more 'friends', but has 'acquaintances' with whom he 'associates', particularly useful acquaintances. He involves himself in politics, either professionally or to augment a good and logical programme. (The fact that marriage partners may choose diametrically opposed parties proves yet again that logic is not tied to the content of that which is judged logically.)

In their twenties gifted individuals may achieve records without too much trouble. In the mid-thirties such exceptional performances must be made in work which demands perseverance and persistence. We know that Richard Wagner said of himself that he had had all his musical inspirations before he was twenty-eight. Yet he still needed years of work to process so many themes until they reached the stage at which they could be translated into musical works. The same goes for scientific and academic work, and in commerce and industry, too, the almost unimaginable reserves of strength which young managers can bring to bear are often vital to the smooth running of a company.

Comprehensive and thorough research has been conducted into the productivity of all these people. It confirms that the peak of productivity lies between 30 and 40, tending towards the middle thirties (see Martha Moers, *Die Entwicklungsphasen* ..., pp. 60–62).

The individual in his thirties is always inclined (relatively speaking, again) to set himself up as something exclusive. Here am I—and there is the world to be conquered, cared for, changed, fought or feared. Each yearning for power starts from an exclusive position, with the danger of the scapegoat psychology: the blame always rests with others—if they could only be eliminated or organized out of the way, the problem would be solved. At this stage in life, being acknowledged to be in the right is more important than *being* in the right.

5. The Second Half of the Thirties

For most people the time that leads into the early forties is a period of continuation of the attitudes to life and the self-assurance which they acquired during the first half of their thirties. In many private conversations, but also in group discussion, I have heard it expressed thus: 'I know what's on the market; I have finished with the romanticism of my twenties; I have become a realist; in this world all that matters is what you are capable of and whether you are in a position to actually push through what you are capable of and what you know,' or: 'I have marked out the path I'm going to take — another three years here and then I'm getting out, to a more senior position in a smaller organization,' or: 'I know my limitations, and I'm going to make sure I don't overstep them — the Peter Principle is not for me, I'm all right where I am; the overall rise in the standard of living will mean that I benefit as much as the rest.'

And then the incomprehensible happens: into the middle of this world of assurance and planning there creeps a doubt, 'as a thief in the night'. And indeed, it usually *is* in the night. You wake up and can't get back to sleep. The events of everyday life run through your head: little irritations and things that have gone wrong stir up the emotions; you decide to tell so-and-so exactly what you think of him. Then drowsiness sets in, and suddenly you are obsessed: 'I'm nearly 40 — 25 years to retirement — my God, another 25 years of the same old grind! *I* know there's nothing new to be expected — at the most new scenery for the same old problem . . . 25 *years* . . . Is there really anything new still to come? In my marriage, for example? We're used to each other by now; things are no worse with us than with everyone else, but can there be anything *new* to come, in *this* marriage? Or at work? I know what I can expect *there* — nothing much! Where, then? Should I start a new hobby? Shall I buy that sailing dinghy after all?'

The next morning it has all gone and life is as usual.

But moments like these return — and now they come during the day as well, even in the middle of a conference. Suddenly you can't keep your thoughts on the matter at hand.

If the man cautiously broaches the subject at home, his wife says she thinks he ought to see the doctor — he must be overworked. What else do you expect if you lead such a life? But the doctor finds nothing unusual, and just says a few wise words about not getting over-excited and the danger of coronary disease and so on and so on.

'*He* can talk. Can *he* see to it that there's less tension after this latest merger, when everyone's gone mad and fears for his job?' 'The young fellows are perfectly ready to take over.'

But the process may take a different course. The man is happy in his job, to which there are many social and cultural aspects, and in his family. His friendship with his own children and with their friends means that there are always young people about the house—it's enough to make you young yourself! Then, suddenly, he is filled with the absurd thought: 'if only I knew what I was *really* put into this world to do!' Again it is the wife who reassures him: 'You need a holiday, let's go out for the evening, then everything will look different again. You like your work, don't you, you don't want to change it for something else?' Again, after the holiday things go better again, yet ... the worm of uncertainty continues to gnaw, and the noise it makes becomes ever louder as soon as things have quietened down inside...

These are just a few of the possible turns of events which may be termed the *crisis of values*, the transition to a new phase. The thirties have operated successfully within a particular system of values. Everything went well, or was at least capable of solution, as long as that system of values was operative. And it looked as if it was the final and only true value system.

Now if this system of values itself should begin to totter — if suddenly the target to which one has aspired, seemingly so desirable, should become hollow and empty, without producing the satisfaction which it had seemed to promise—then one is truly lost! The fear of losing one's way may be pushed back, like a threatening spectre, into the

unconscious mind, where it can be locked up; or its presence can be drowned by continually increasing the work-
load, or by having a stiff drink, or by going in search of
erotic adventure — or by allowing oneself, in a half-sleep, to
be kept 'busy' in front of the television screen . . .

But the fear which has been apparently suppressed in the
subconscious remains active none the less. In a typical
conversation with a 42-year-old manager of a business
which he had built up himself, this found expression in the
following terms: 'You know I had to start the business on
borrowed capital. I've worked hard for 12 years now to pay
off that debt. And all the time I've had a sort of picture in
front of me: when I stop owing people money, I thought,
that's when life *really begins* — I shall be independent — I'll
throw a massive party. I reached that stage last week, but
instead of being in a party mood I've been in a state of deep
depression ever since. Now I've got to spend another 30
years in the same old office dealing with the same old
problems, and now I haven't even got the idea of making
myself independent to spur me on . . . What do you think,
shall I just sell the business and start again somewhere else?
Then at least I'll have something to live for!'

Seeking refuge elsewhere, however, is not going: for *you
take yourself with you*. You're never going to go back to being
19, and you will never escape the crisis of values, even if
you manage to cover it up for some time. There is no
objection to doing something else, as long as you have first
succeeded in *doing the same thing in a different way* — and then
it is often no longer necessary to change jobs.

'Doing the same thing in a different way' means first and
foremost finding new values 'to live for'. They must come
from an atmosphere of spiritual interest. This is why Martha Moers speaks of the problems of these years as the
development of 'spiritual-mental strivings'. Rudolf Steiner
speaks here of developing the consciousness soul, of
becoming aware of our spiritual personality, in the sphere

of thinking, feeling and willing. It is a problem of the will, to which an appeal is made.

The intellect is dependent on the values within which one wishes to order phenomena. The German surgeon Sauerbruch expressed this in his own way with the words: '*Der Verstand ist eine Dirne, bei der man jedes Geisteskind zeugen kann*' (The intellect is a whore in whom we can beget any brain-child). The values themselves are determined by the will, which makes the choice and cuts the knot.

I have said before that the beginning of the forties is a sort of fork in the road leading to the rest of our lives. Either the road goes downhill, together with the biological functions of the body and mind, or it leads into totally new territory in which quite different creative powers are awakened. These may make possible a second peak in the individual's powers of creation, the zenith of which lies in the second half of the fifties and may endure until far into the seventies, though there is generally a clear decline during the second half of the sixties. It must be asked whether in many cases this possibility is not culturally influenced by the role in which retired people are put in our society.

If we review again the whole of the 'middle phase of life', the period between 21 and 42, then we may distinguish three main periods, each of which has its own dominant feature: (1) the development of the sentient soul with its driving force in the vital-mental strivings; this is the time of *Himmelhoch jauch-zend – zum Tode betrübt*. It is the period of expansion and self-investigation, of starting a family and changing jobs; (2) the development of the intellectual soul, the period in which the 'objective strivings' are dominant, the time of great activities and achievements in an objective system of values; (3) the development of the consciousness soul, the time of the incipient breakthrough of the 'spiritual-mental strivings', a period which begins to upset the assurance and security of the previous objective period and opens up the way for a fertile entering into a completely new and great phase of life: *the third main phase of life, the phase of mature and fully developed human existence.*

Guardini, as we have seen, points out that no phase of life is superior or inferior to any other. In each phase of life man can be wholly that which he can be *at that time.* The child, including the adolescent, is not a 'not yet adult person' but rather a child, with his own particular task of development, one which is just as important as the task of the fifties in the total span of the individual's life. Both can sleep away their tasks and possibilities or they can realize them, yet one is just as important as the other.

In the middle phase of life, between about 21 and 42, the character is formed by meeting the resistance of reality. The price is paid in the process of sobering and of objectification. After this period it is a matter of seeing whether other, new values can be found.

6. The Third Main Phase of Life – the Forties

Biological decline and possible spiritual development
We ended the description of the problems in the middle phase of life with the words: 'it is a matter of seeing whether other, new values can be found'. However, we shall see that this task is not so easy.

In the middle phase, after all, we still had the current with us. In our western culture it is more or less inevitable that we come across material (intellectual) values and incorporate them into our lives. Our entire culture is still one of the intellectual soul, with in some cases, such as science and technology, the beginnings of cultural values based on self-conscious awareness.

Our civilization is on the threshold of exploring new, self-discovered, spiritual values. The old spiritual values from the magical-mythological past have become impoverished in rationalism and extinguished by materialism. If we are again to make of religion something that is alive—and that is of vital importance for the social relationships between people—then the old hierarchical rule of spiritual values will have to make way for the independent search for and creation of a new hierarchy from the bottom upwards. It is no longer someone else who decides what is spiritually good for us; instead, we ourselves seek a teacher, either in literature or in the flesh, whom we will recognize to be our spiritual instructor, and from whom we will learn until we move on.

That during this process old concepts can acquire a new reality is a discovery which will be made by many.

New values which have yet to be found are existential values. That is to say, we not only accept or 'support' them as theory, we also 'are' them. As soon as we go in search of our higher Self we find ourselves in a world of spiritual realities and every psychic quality becomes a force with which we must struggle in order to appropriate it or to vanquish it. Each spiritual step then becomes an entry into a new landscape, as it is called by the phenomenologists, with new encounters which, especially in the initial stages, need not necessarily be of a friendly nature.

The third main phase of life (according to the Chinese, the phase in which we acquire wisdom) begins in the forties, or, in my presentation, around the age of 42. But development may fluctuate on either side of this mean.

This phase of life begins with considerable turbulence. Biologically, it betokens the beginning of the declining life-force. For women it is clearly marked as the end of the physically creative phase. For men it is a phase of heightened sexual needs, which are generally misunderstood by their wives. Psychologically, these years signify a period of doubt, disorientation and tendencies towards illusory solutions, with brief periods of happiness. Spiritually, these years mean wrestling with the emptiness, with the sense of having lost all the old ground and not yet having found any new.

The reaction to this state of affairs can vary enormously. For many who are unprepared the situation is a shock and a proof of weakness, and must be pushed aside by working even harder, or by chasing even more grimly after a dynamic career with ever-widening horizons — or by anaesthetizing the voices of weakness and doubt with alcohol, sexual adventures, or sitting passively in front of the television. Sometimes we also look for a scapegoat to blame for the souring of our *joie de vivre* in our wives or husbands or in our superiors or children. For the husband it is the familiar story of 'Mary doesn't understand me any more', for the wife 'John has lost interest in me'. This can develop into experience of the double of oneself and those close to one. (More of this later.)

In the path of life we now find ourselves faced by a crossroads; the choice we make determines the future course of our lives and whether a new leitmotiv will be realizable or whether it will disappear into the depths of the subconscious, from where, for the rest of our lives, it will present a constant threat to our feeling of self-respect. What had already made its appearance at the end of the thirties, namely, the doubt about the enduring value of the expansive, I-centred approach to life, now becomes an existential problem.

For whoever has not sought after non-material values in life this situation is threatening in the extreme. The discovery of declining vitality, the increasing difficulty with which we do and decide things, coupled with a vague dissatisfaction with our own situation, is an attack on our experience of the ego, on our sense of self-respect.

It is understandable that Martha Moers says that what she calls the fourth phase of life (42 to 56 years) has a disposition towards crisis. She draws an analogy with puberty, which is also preceded by a period of assurance, abruptly terminated by the discovery that we know neither ourselves nor life. But the great difference is that our first puberty occurs during an ascendant life-line, while the second occurs during a descendant one. Although in both cases the former harmony of life is in jeopardy, the essence of the crisis is now quite a different one: then it was a break-through, with power, into the reality of 'life'; now, with reduction in power, it is a growing uncertainty about the value of that same 'life'.

The reduction in drive is caused by the start of the involution process of all the tissues in the body. Each organ in the human body has its own life curve. In certain organs, such as the sensory organs and the organs of internal secretion, it is possible to measure the pattern of change with some accuracy, and a considerable amount is therefore known about it. For other organs, such as the nervous system and those which regulate the metabolism, the results of research rather tend to vary.

The best known manifestation of this decline is the hardening of tissue in the eye, resulting in an inability of the lens to adjust and leading to difficulty in focusing for reading. It is in our forties that many of us find that we need reading-glasses for precision work at close range. Our own experience, again, is sufficient to tell us that lung tissue becomes less supple at this age; when we have to run to catch a bus or train, we need much longer to regain our breath than in our youth. The entire muscular system, too, loses strength and flexibility, so that, particularly because of the loss of flexibility, older people need more energy for the same physical performance. The change takes place gradually, but is usually discovered quite suddenly when a particular situation reveals a hitherto hidden shortcoming. The most important and at the same time the best known of these changes is that which takes place in internal secre-tions. The endocrine glands in both men and women begin to cease functioning, but the course which this process takes is extremely different in the two sexes. (We shall discuss the significance of the female and male menopause in marriage in a separate chapter.)

In her book *The Seven Ages of Woman* the renowned American gynaecologist Elizabeth Parker has described woman's life in her struggle with her physical life curve and also (a contribution which is rarely found) brings psychological and spiritual development into her discussion. She describes the menopause in its many forms in three phases: pre-menopause, menopause, post-menopause.

In the pre-menopause a woman may complain: 'I don't know what it is. I'm not really ill, I just don't feel well. I'm nervous and irritable—my family find me difficult. Little things can make me go wild, and then again I have to cry. I've lost all the joy of life—I'm worried about myself.' Another woman may have bodily complaints: a stiff back, shooting or nagging pains in arms or legs causing sleeplessness. Others again have headaches, which they never had before, or swollen joints, especially in the fingers. Yet others wonder whether they might not have a 'heart condition', because one night they have suddenly had an attack of palpitations (it is interesting that attacks of palpitations can also be a manifestation of the male menopause, but ten years later).

These symptoms are the result of a shift in the hormone balance maintained by the organs of internal secretion. The function of the ovaries begins to fall off, menstruation becomes irregular, with either reduced or, on the contrary, greatly increased symptoms. The failure to produce the female hormone (the oestrogens) stimulates the pituitary gland into greater activity and this in turn has an effect on the thyroid and adrenal glands. In short, the old equilibrium is lost and it is several years before a new equilibrium has established itself. It is at that moment that all menopausal symptoms disappear. The woman feels reborn and experiences new, sometimes uninhibited, energy for living.

The male menopause takes a different course. The heightened sexual needs of men may be regarded as a manifestation of pre-menopause which generally occurs in the mid-forties. The mental unrest accompanying it is probably influenced by the same hormonal changes. Otherwise, however, the male menopause progresses far more slowly, and it is assumed that it is not complete as an involution until well into the second half of the fifties. The physical symptoms are accompanied by a lack of stability in emotional life; sudden watering of the eyes or a lump in the throat when something touches the emotions; and attacks of palpitations (tachycardia) which last from a few minutes up to a quarter of an hour and cause considerable mental shock, since in men they generally occur during the day in the middle of work and give the impression of being a threat to the victim's life (which they are not). In view of the high percentage of heart attacks suffered between the ages of 45 and 60 it is understandable that a tachycardiac attack should make a considerable impression on the patient as well as on his environment. The safest course after such an attack is nevertheless to see a doctor for a heart check-up.

The actual hormone involution can then last another 10 or 20 years. One of the consequences is the 'old man's complaint', the prostate swelling that appears when testicular function ceases. Another unpleasant side-effect is that with the hormonal decline of the reproductive glands older men can sometimes be troubled by sexual fantasies occurring mainly just before falling asleep and just before waking. For some men these fantasies can become an obsession precisely because morally the person in question condemns them. Such men will only talk about their problem in highly confidential conversation. Luckily there is a fast medicinal cure available. What one might call a monument to this problem is to be found in the Old Testament when Suzanna is spied upon by the elders. These were not the least among the people and nevertheless . . . !

With this we find ourselves — side-tracked by our discussion of the male menopause — involved in the problems of a much later phase of life. It will have become clear by now that in the forties we can speak only of a male pre-menopause, and that during these years the problems which men encounter are on the psychological and particularly spiritual planes. In the psyche there is the conflict between a longing to be young again, to start again at 20 and relive the entire expansive phase, only this time better, with the help of the experience gained the first time round, and on the other hand the wish to push on through to the real business of life, the realization of one's own leitmotiv, to certainty in a spiritual reality in which we can live up to our higher ego.

The desire to be young again (as camouflage for the inner longing for something new in life) can lead to external projection of these needs. Many men suddenly start to wear dashing, young styles of clothing, to walk spryly, to try to be the life-and-soul of the party, and so on. Something of the rooster in the man becomes visible.

But women, too, suddenly start going to the beauty salon for rejuvenation. They hope that they will be taken for their daughters' elder sisters. The illusion of starting again at 20 must, of course, have eventual repercussions, even though there are men and women who are capable of maintaining the illusion for a very long time. The point, as Jung says, is to tear oneself free from the exaggerated 'ego-imprison-ment', the *Ichverhaftung*. A restructuring which I call 'spiritual maturation' is called for. This process is coupled with a different way of experiencing *time*. Until the age of 40 we have only a future; everything is still possible, reality is still to come. Now, however, that future acquires a horizon: 25 years to retirement and then what? Moreover, time passes faster and faster, as against a past which grows longer and longer. The contribution made by the will to work becomes increasingly weak (we need to make more effort to achieve the same result), especially for work with a rapidly changing content. Interest in work in which knowledge, experience of life and the ability to form judgements play a part increases — and in the later years of this phase this applies especially to creative work, for higher achievements of a complex spiritual nature. This is true for all levels of work and must become the basis for a healthy staffing policy during these years. (More of this in a separate chapter.)

The process that Jung calls 'freeing oneself from ego-imprisonment' is described by Martha Moers in the following terms: 'Too much ego-bound, guided by assertiveness and the drive for power, and aimed at the utility aspect, shortly before approaching old age, man reaches the crisis of the turning-point in his life. Having overcome that, we must then make the final decision as to how we are going to go on to meet the conclusion of our lives.'

It is precisely people whose work is of a more spiritual nature — artists, for example, and political leaders — who only now really get into their stride and experience the fifties as the beginning of a truly creative phase. Hence Lehmann's description of these years after the crisis as 'the age of the eminent leaders'.

Particularly for those who have to work with young people — teachers and lecturers, for example — the crisis years are a severely testing time. Those who come through and free themselves of their ego-imprisonment go on to become leaders accepted by the young people; those who fail in this have also failed in the eyes of the young, who have a nice sense for the genuineness of a person or for the neurotic, the clinging to position, to knowledge or prestige. Thus if the forties are not the last chance, they nevertheless constitute a special period with significant possibilities for maturation.

'At no later time of life is the psychological constellation again so favourable for a far-reaching freeing from all too great an ego-imprisonment and thereby also for the development of true sympathy and unselfish willingness to help as now,' says Martha Moers.

Here I should like to interpose a brief reminder of the differences that we established earlier between biological drives, psychological needs or desires and spiritual ambitions or directions of the will. In the human soul, forces enter from two sides and encounter one another in the experience of one's own being: instinct or drive 'from below', and ambition or aspiration 'from above'.

In the middle phase of life all drives had to be encountered by the ego and confronted in the soul by higher aspirations. The result is the development of a number of aspects of the human soul which, following Rudolf Steiner, I have called the sentient, intellectual and consciousness souls.

In the forties all these aspects of the human psyche are available to serve the life which has yet to be lived. The main question is then: What do I want to use them for? What, now, have I actually got to do in this life? What is my real task?

A personal word or two may not be out of place. Ever since I was 30 I had occupied myself with the theoretical side of these questions. I knew exactly what was to come and thought I should come through the crisis, when it came, with flying colours. The reality turned out differently. Knowledge of things does not free one from living through them and suffering through them when the time comes. For several years I often lay awake half the night thinking of what I really ought to do, and where my true life's work lay. Yet I had an interesting job as a child psychiatrist and as the director of a large institution for the education of disturbed children — work which I had started myself and in which I was surrounded by valuable assistants and colleagues. And yet! The answer came from so unexpected a quarter that I should never have been able to think of it myself. The call came from industry to involve myself with young unskilled factory workers and later with the training and the organization of their work. With hindsight, I realize that this was my real leitmotiv — but others had to put the question to me before I could recognize my own task. The fact that I had been waiting for this through many years of inner doubt made my enthusiasm for my new work even greater.

I have found that in very many cases the demand comes from outside but remains unheard unless one is ready for it. Reaching maturity is a process which no one is spared, not even those who know about it. Nevertheless, knowing about the crisis of the forties has one great advantage: you know that you and you alone are involved, so that you do not make the mistake of looking for scapegoats or adverse forces in your surroundings or circumstances. Here Künkel's phrase is very apt: '*Das Schicksal kommt von Innen*' ('Our lot comes from within') — even if I hear it in the world outside!

7. *The Beginning of the Fifties*

At the end of the forties the intensity of the crisis lessens. It now emerges whether or not the individual has found something new. If not, the phases still to follow become a tragically declining line of life. The individual clings increasingly to his work. Every capable younger man, still in his expansionary phase, becomes a threat. It becomes increasingly necessary to the individual to 'stand on his stripes', that is, to insist upon the supposed authority of his nominal position. He is no longer capable of using and accommodating himself to new situations. His own past and experience of life are idealized. The young of today are a lot of good-for-nothings, they're coddled, they earn too much, they're cheeky and rude, they lack respect. (The same story, in other words, as may be read in the inscription in the pyramids.)

The man who goes on in this vein says very little indeed about young people but a very great deal about his own tragic position. At work, such people are a ball and chain round the leg of their organization. For example, in an administrative organization there was a departmental head in his mid-fifties who was in the habit of arriving ten minutes early every morning and then looking at his watch every time one of his staff came in for the morning's work. On Monday mornings, however, he would come in ten minutes later. Then he would take a great wad of files from his brief-case and deposit them noisily on his desk, with the words: 'Oh yes, gentlemen, by all means spend the week-end quietly at home. If I didn't take my work home with me we should never be through here.' And they would all nod in agreement and say: 'Yes, Mr Smith.' And when he had turned his back, they would point significantly to their foreheads.

The attitude of 'I'm still here, you can't walk over me, I'm in charge for a few more years yet' also points to a powerless attempt to prop up an authority which has in effect ceased to exist long since. Nevertheless, it is well that we ask ourselves whether this sort of situation is really necessary in a well-run organization with the right staffing policy. I shall return to this later.

For the man who has come through his crisis of the forties, the fifties are a liberation. The horizon expands, new problems of wider significance become apparent. Life becomes more interesting, the distance to little everyday problems increases. Interest in the thinking behind policies is awakened, and there is a new and deeply felt joy in seeing young people growing in their expansionary phase. The overall result of this is that this person can give advice and support in a completely new way, and that he is accepted. As already pointed out, this is of paramount importance in those professions in which young people receive their training or education.

New creativity breaks through; if at the age of 35 one was a gifted barrister or an active boss, now one becomes an eminent jurist or a wise and mild manager. For the man who is continuing to grow mentally and spiritually, the middle of the fifties is a second peak in his creative life. He has already been able to review and order his experience, but he still has the vitality to express this order in his work. This is the age of the 'eminent leader'.

For the woman, too, there are two paths open. The negative path is reflected in the woman thus. Now that the menopause is over, her vitality has returned, often in greater measure than before. But she has found no new outlet for it, and complains: 'I've never had any time for myself. I've always been there to help the family, I've slaved away from morning till night. I've never had time to do any reading, and if I did I was always too tired even to pick up a book. Now it's too late. The children have left home, my husband is engrossed in his work, and I'm left here empty-handed.' And in furious activity she throws herself at the housekeeping, cleaning things that are already clean, dusting where there is no dust, tyrannizing anybody who gets near enough, everlastingly complaining that she is the victim of the mountains of work that she has to get through.

There is a bitter and cynical story that illustrates this state of affairs. A man in his early sixties had died suddenly. When the will came to be read it emerged that the dead man's last wish was that he should be cremated and that his ashes should then be sprinkled over the carpet in the sitting room. The years of misery which must have gone before can only be guessed at.

From my own experience I am familiar with the situation of the older woman in a profession, such as the matron at a hospital. Here again there are two possibilities: there is the kind of matron who takes out her own bitterness on the student nurses, and the matron who guides them as a mother would, and in whose hospital there is always an atmosphere of happiness and joy among the nurses at work.

In such arduous professions as teaching and nursing it is

only right that the woman who has had a long professional career should be able to retire at 60 so that she has enough time and energy to build up a new life for herself after her professional life has ended. Happily, this situation prevails in many countries.

But in contrast to the hospital dragon and the woman ferociously and bitterly engrossed in her work there are also women who come through the crisis of the menopause with a positive outlook on life and joyfully find that they can again tackle all sorts of things and that they can at least realize a new aspect of their leitmotiv. Grateful for the past phase in which they have been able to be useful to others, they now find a new task in social life, or they take up gardening with fresh enthusiasm, or return to a long-since forgotten musical instrument. And with modesty and *élan* she will assuredly immerse herself in her new task as a grandmother, creating a second generation in which they can feel safe and warm and where they can hear stories which come alive as nowhere else.

8. After 56

But the development of the individual has still not ended. At about the age of 56 (it is remarkable how consistently this figure recurs in research reports) new clouds begin to form on the horizon. The high plateau on which life unrolled provided a good view in all directions, but it was chiefly a view directed at the outside world. The gaze is now again turned inwards. It is as though all the values of life must be relived existentially. (Rümke and Charlotte Bühler refer to a *pre-senium*, a pre-old-age, and place the emphasis on the confrontation with the end of life, now genuinely in sight, or at least the confrontation with the reality of retirement.) My own tendency would be to see the whole problem in rather broader terms, even if it is certain that the confrontation with the end and with a final judgement plays a part.

It is possible that a feeling arises of a difficult new period. Yet again everything has to pass through what Goethe calls *Stirb und werde*—literally, 'die and become'. Not that the values which have been found are beginning to totter, to become somewhat shaky, but it becomes clear that they are not yet truly in our possession. If we ask ourselves in all honesty, 'What would I really be able to take through the gates of death as the fruits of my life?' then much of what is now bound up with knowledge, status and experience would have to be abandoned. Some people experience the beginning of this period as a premonition of yet greater trials, others see it as a series of tasks to be expected with which they would rather not be confronted. For the man, too, his profession often produces a number of disillusions. Anyone who has reached the age of 60 is regarded as 'doing the rest of his time', even if he is still doing his job perfectly and to everyone's satisfaction. Yet again he has to reconcile himself to abdicating from what he has built up himself and which will certainly be continued on different lines by those who follow. This detachment is only now turning into reality; hitherto it has been no more than theory.

It is now high time to prepare for what one still hopes to achieve, what one will have to drop, and what one may still be able to finish. There is a growing anxious realization that this is less than one had thought up to now. The past passes in review. It is incredible that one has wasted so much precious time on trifles—if only I had more time *before* me, time which I let slip through my hands like sand! There is no longer a long future for me in this life, but what, despite this, might prove to be enduring?

In a certain sense the development of the individual's life has come to a temporary conclusion at the age of 63. Toddler, schoolchild and adolescent—together they make up the youth in which so much was granted us. And as usual the gift of the world is always a mixture of joy and sorrow, of helping and hindering experience. Vital-mental, objective and spiritual strivings have made of the expansionary phase a period in which much could be given to the world in the form of work, friendship and enmity, commanding and obeying, but in which it was also possible and necessary to interiorize and appropriate past experiences. We emerged from this expansionary phase as mature personalities knowing what we wanted and knowing what we were worth.

Crisis and involution, the peak in the fifties and yet again the final test have made us the mature person who has developed a sense of the difference between cleverness and wisdom, between proud ability and modesty. A final period before the age of patriarchs enables us to draw up the balance and accommodate ourselves to the fact of old age with restraint and acquiescence, but also with extreme inner activity which will finally be able to lead to goodness — but also with declining powers and with physical infirmities and dependence upon others. Shall we have to learn to live with our own decay, or shall we be allowed to die in good health? These are very real questions for those preparing for the period of old age.

I am not able to speak of the final phase of life itself. Who can speak with authority about a phase of life through which he has not yet passed, and been able to compare his own experiences with the many experiences of others, acquired in friendly or therapeutic discussion? However, from letters and conversations with the very old it does emerge that the final years of life are experienced in many different ways. One old man, far into his eighties, writes that total dependence has led him to a final righting of his account, and a new, deep awareness of the reality of the words: 'Christ is in me.' For others it is a matter of desperately clinging to a life which is gradually slipping away.

It is a well-known fact that creativity at an advanced age

is not impossible. In America some 20 years ago Grandma Moses, a woman who started painting when she was almost 80, was a great success at exhibitions and in magazine articles. And many have since followed in her footsteps, with varying degrees of outward success but in every case with enormous inner gain.

In his old age Goethe described the phases of life in these terms: the child is a realist, the young man an idealist, the man a sceptic, the old man a mystic!

It is important that we make every possible effort to help old people have a creative and fertile evening to their lives. Just as we have referred to a family culture for young children, so there ought to be a home culture for the aged. The homes in which they live should be centres of culture, with lectures, musical evenings and creative courses, in which other local people ought to be able to take part. This would work both ways: the local people would have a centre in which interesting things are happening, and the old people would maintain their contact with a living world. It is again a well-known fact that old people who lead an active life enjoy better health than those who vegetate in front of the television or the radio. We know that many great artists produce their best work long after they have passed their seventieth birthday. The famous Japanese painter Hokusai is said to have declared that everything he did before he was 73 was quite worthless and that it was only then that he had embarked on his true artistic career. Titian painted his most powerful works when he was almost a hundred. Verdi, Richard Strauss, Schütz, Sibelius and others continued to compose music until they were over 80. The list of composers who were active until their late seventies is too long to be included here. In every field, writers, painters and musicians have been able to carry on working far longer than scientists and businessmen. That this is so is a result of the fact that with increasing age the path that leads inwards progresses ever further, while perception of what goes on outside declines. I have been struck by the fact that in the more elderly businessmen whom I have known—people who wanted to carry on working as long as possible—intelligence and routine persist for far longer than the ability to *assess new external situations*. This has taken many a successfully established company to the brink of bankruptcy and beyond.

If we consider the achievements of humanity we see that the wisdom of old age can reveal itself in a timeless world. Here lies the field which is attainable for everybody who remains active: the summation of the essence of life and the finding of a timeless world of values and meaningfulness!

Chapter Three

Male and Female Development – Marriage

During International Women's Year (1975), in which so much emphasis was laid on woman's equality, the confusion surrounding that equality, or lack of it, increased rather than diminished. My starting-point in this chapter will be the spiritual equality of men and women — that is, equality at the ego level. Both men and women are people and as such possess an ego identity, and it is this that increasingly determines the path taken by the individual's development throughout the course of life, regardless of sex.

At the same time, one would need to be blind to try to deny the biological differences between the two sexes. Biologically, men and women are each other's complement; they need one another, as is the case with all higher forms of life, in order to secure the continued existence of the species.

As the content of mental life is determined by the influence of the *bios* or biological forces and the spirit there is also a difference between male and female mental awareness.

In the minds of men and women two different force-fields play a part. From within the biological drives various impulses and longings penetrate the soul — from within the spiritual strivings there is *in equal measure* a problem of individuation. Since the human being is a trinity of body, psyche and spirit, the spiritual path, of individuation, will follow different paths in men and women. At the same time, each individual is unique and equal, even where there are differences in the level of spiritual development and moral quality. *Where* the individual is along the path of development does not determine the value of the individuality, just as an old man is not superior or inferior to a child. The person who has acquired a certain insight has more responsibility in his wrestling with moral and social problems and problems of knowledge. It is for this reason that I talk of the equivalence of individualities as beings with aspirations. As I have said elsewhere: 'The human mind is a citizen of two worlds, a spiritual one and a biological one.' Because of the latter the soul-life of men and women differs.

During his long and rich life the depth psychologist Carl Gustav Jung recorded his own soul-life and that of his many patients in their dreams and in the waking state. A subtle observer, he was always at pains to observe phenomena without the tinted spectacles of a theory or system, as he was otherwise afraid that he might see certain phenomena sharply but completely miss others. He wanted to be and remain a psychologist, not a theologian or a philosopher. Many of his critics have accused him of a lack of system, and find it difficult to find their way in the vast sea of knowledge that he uncovered. It did not escape his observant eye that men and women are not only each other's complement but also that in the depth of his mind every man finds a female structure and vice versa. These he called the man's anima and the woman's animus.

Man, built biologically for externalized activity, for conquering and subjugating, has in his anima the regulating factor which may appear to him in dreams in the image of a female being which stands in his way and makes clear to him that he is in danger of forgetting his real leitmotiv.

The anima-animus is quite a different thing from the coarsely biological Oedipus complex. The anima is in the service of strivings, of which I have described three levels when discussing the human life-path. This service means determining norms and stimulating further development on the path of the leitmotiv.

In his works Jung gives numerous examples of powerful anima-animus dreams which often recur until their judgement has been understood.

Biologically, man is constructed on a bisexual framework. The primitive kidney which lays down the entire urogenital system during the early embryonic period develops, for a time, both organ systems, until there comes a moment when maleness or femaleness gains the upper hand and the organs of the opposite sex cease development. In the adult man and woman it is possible to see the remains of the embryonic organs of the opposite sex. For instance the mammary glands are initially present in both man and woman, but only develop fully in the female.

The potential which does not find expression in physical terms remains in existence and has an influence on the mind — not in the form of hormonal effects and physical-biological drives and stimuli, but rather in the deeper levels of the subconscious. Here Jung distinguishes three different levels:

1. The personal subconcious — our memories and forgotten impressions, and complexes acquired during life
2. The collective subconscious — emotions and invasions common to whole groups such as peoples and races
3. The archetypes which have the character of humanity and which in their language of imagery are the same throughout the world.

The archetypes become susceptible of experience in symbols; they recur in all religions and in many fairy-tales. Because of their human character they also have what Jung calls an animus-character. They have a shocking effect and function also as a conscience, where man threatens to sink below the level of humanity.

One of the most important archetypes is the anima-animus. Where the man in his maleness threatens to become too one-sided and lose his humanity, the anima intervenes with a demand for general humanity; and conversely in the woman. Jung expresses this in different terms. Each Adam, he says, carries his Eve within himself, and every Eve her

Adam. On earth each seeks a meeting with the fellow being who looks like his or her own Eve or Adam, so that they will remain in spiritual equilibrium. It is the Gretchen who after her death accompanies Faust on his way, and the dead Beatrice who can lead Dante through the highest spheres. Goethe's *Faust* ends with the 'Chorus mysticus': '*Das Ewig-Weibliche zieht uns hinan*' – 'The eternal feminine lifts us above'.

In puberty the individual awakens not only to an inner awareness of his own sex and to curiosity towards his fellow beings, but also, particularly in the years that follow, to the first awareness of his own anima-animus. In early adolescence there is a homo-erotic phase. The young boy experiences his own femaleness in himself and seeks his inner equilibrium in a hero-worship relationship with a male object. This is the period in which girls have a crush on a teacher while boys find an older man for their feelings of reverence. All this may take place in the banal world of football heroes and film stars, but it may also express itself in highly refined and intimate daydream experiences.

As adolescence progresses, there comes the mental awakening for the opposite sex, eroticism. It is precisely this eroticism which is reinforced by the search for the individual's own Eve or Adam in the encounter with the opposite sex.

The transition from homosexuality to heterosexuality is a normal part of development and it is understandable that in this phase of transition disturbances of the normal pattern may arise. If the individual's first sexual experiences are repellent or aggressive this may lead to fixation in homosexuality. Whether the ultimate result of this is true homosexuality is then chiefly a matter of other encounters.

The problems of homosexuality are extremely complex. In the 1930s I saw quite a few artists in my psychotherapeutic practice, and learnt to see the homoerotic component in the human soul in the light of those who pay more attention to what comes up from within themselves than to what the hard, factual world does to affect them. In the 1950s, as a psychiatrist treating students, I became acquainted chiefly with homosexuality in adolescence.

Personally, I am inclined to distinguish between biological homosexuality which in extreme cases becomes apparent in quite early youth and the mental homoeroticism which is bound up with the discovery of the individual's own anima-animus existence.

Every human being possesses within him his own biological duality, alongside the chromosomes which are probably partly instrumental in causing one half of the duality to prevail. (I say 'probably partly' because I have learnt to be cautious about thinking in mechanical cause-and-effect sequences when considering the phenomena of life. After all, in this sort of terrain, what is really cause and what is the instrument of a supreme ordering principle? A violin cannot produce a sonata even if it is indispensable in its playing.)

The awareness of this duality, besides the elaboration of one possibility together with the retardation of the other, leads to varying experiences of the individual's own 'being-situation'. To put it in popular terms, there are men (and conversely women) who are 90 per cent man and 10 per cent woman — they are the undisputed he-men. There are men (and conversely women) who experience themselves as being 10 per cent man and 90 per cent woman — they are the true homosexuals. In between, all sorts of gradations are possible, 60–40, 50–50, 40–60, and so on. In this last group, the individual's experience of himself varies in different encounters. In general it may be said that those with a strongly one-sided nature have to pay for their certainty with a simplification of their capacity for inner experience, and that a more even distribution of experience leads to enrichment of the mind.

I shall return to these problems when we discuss interpersonal relations in marriage during the various phases of life. In the 'man'-man and 'woman'-woman the foregoing plays an important part. The completely mannish man and womanly woman are so tied to their own world that they can develop no feeling for the fact of their partner's being different. They are not so much egotists as colour-blind to other types of mental self-awareness. They are only able to understand their partners with that part of their own souls which is female or male respectively. Completely one-sided people in this respect always make a somewhat infantile impression on others, and they suffer from the fact that they are always addressed first in regard to their sex and only then in regard to their personality.

The psychiatrist dealing with students has to do with the insecure phase of adolescence, in which the young person whose feelings are unfolding wonders (far more often than most people think) whether he is really 'normal', or whether he might not perhaps be homosexual. Only in a joint careful reading of the nature of the individual's experiences is it possible to help him towards self-insight in what is for him a matter of vital importance. A single incautious word can have a suggestive influence and perpetuate an inner uncertainty which might otherwise equally well have been resolved. On the other hand admitting to oneself that one is a homosexual is the first step along the way to finding one's own path through life, one's own leitmotiv in a heterosexual world.

It is a step in the right direction that it is now possible to speak of these matters openly. But it is equally true to say that the distorted, cramped fashion in which certain homosexuals believe they must fight for their rights says more about their own tolerance of frustration than about the problem of homosexuality itself – which is never simply black and white, but is always built up from a rich spectrum of colours between black and white. The same applies to women's emancipation. There too, polarizing simplification does not assist true emancipation in the many shades of 'being a woman'.

After this introduction in which I have tried to place the issue of maleness and femaleness in perspective, it is possible for us to examine the evolution from sex through eroticism to love, as the basis for the evolution of the man-woman relationship through the course of life. (And when I refer to the man-woman relationship, I also mean the woman-man relationship.)

The first discovery by an individual of his own sexuality takes place during pre-puberty. In the girl it is marked by the first menstruation, in the boy by the first erections and night-time ejaculations. At that moment attention is still fixed on the functioning of the individual's own body, but soon afterwards this attention is transferred to the opposite sex. In a healthy environment of non-neurotic forms of social interaction, the life of both boys and girls then follows its usual course. Sport, camping, working and playing together — all these are more essential to the content of the mind than the problems of sex.

After this initial phase considerable differentiation between the various population groups becomes apparent. In my work with young working people it became clear to me how severely the 'gainful' employment of 14, 15 and 16-year-olds hinders the possibilities for the development of sex, eroticism and love. Since truly mind-destroying labour with limited 'freedom of movement', for eight hours a day, becomes the main ingredient of life, the mind is unable to develop and the individual is condemned to grow to adulthood at a puberty level of general development. It is only necessary to watch packers at a conveyor belt or girls in a typing pool to realize that here the soul is being forced to vegetate in a state of semi-wakefulness. The same goes for boys in unskilled labour or involved in work programmed by over-preparation. In the construction and shipbuilding industries, by contrast, where the work is much more varied and more nearly approaches the nature of craftsmanship, opportunities for character development are far greater.

Where the mind has to spend hours every day in a semi-wakeful state doing fatiguing and monotonous work, sexual feelings and fantasies gain the upper hand and distort it. Again, it is only necessary to spend a few moments at a randomly chosen point in the working day listening to the conversation of girls working on a conveyor belt to be moved by the one-sidedness of what fills such girls' minds in such a situation. And when in later adolescence they become engaged and get married, an unconscious but important phase of development has been passed over which is only to a very slight degree capable of being made good. We have good reason to be surprised by the elasticity of human development potential when we see how well many of them come out of it. This, however, does not absolve us of our responsibility to fight for improvement of the opportunities for development of the largest section of the population from generation to generation.

The problems are of course quite different when we consider the privileged position of those young people who are able to complete a full course of secondary education.

But let us return to the adolescent aspect of the man-woman relationship as it may develop in not all too un-favourable circumstances. By this it will be apparent that in the following pages I do not propose to discuss the statistics of what is likely to happen in what are often unfavourable circumstances. Instead, I would describe what follows as a deliberately chosen idealized case.

The adolescent, having accepted his own sexuality and having discovered eroticism in the soul, enters a magical land full of unexpected and breathtaking experiences. Hope and fear, rapture and depression succeed one another, feelings of tenderness and respect begin to unfold, along-side feelings of indignation and repulsion. The whole rainbow of emotions has to be experienced before the individual can become a complete person in the great middle phase of life. He will need the nuances of the powers of the soul which make mutual understanding, acceptance and forgiveness possible. It is in this phase that each individual begins to become aware of both his maleness and his femaleness. Each man seeks his Eve, each woman her Adam. Deep in the soul there is an ideal picture which completes the individual's own soul. Will he meet the right person or will he have to make do with the first one to correspond roughly to the ideal? When the first relationship has been established, it becomes a practice-ground for further development, so that, however it may end, both parties end up richer than when they started. Many people have to have more than one such relationship before the inner security of recognition is created.

Even those who believe in the predestination of two people for each other will have to develop the maturity necessary for the recognition of the future marriage partner. The initial encounter will be distorted if it is restricted too severely to direct sexual relations. The bombardment of coarse sexuality maintained by our communications media, particularly the sex film, has a disturbing influence on the psychological side of maturation. A marriage founded on sexual attraction principally or exclusively will not last long. In fact there is nothing more boring than sex by itself. The possibilities for variety are soon exhausted, and for the soul there is nothing left. Wife-swapping, group sex and the like may provide new but temporary stimulation, but the relationship between two individuals does not thereby become any the deeper, and the person within the person remains unsatisfied and lonely.

While the sentient soul, in which the 'vital-mental strivings' operate, is being explored in the twenties the eroticism discovered during adolescence becomes an experienced reality in the soul. This eroticism, aroused by the encounter with the life partner, can now expand to embrace the relationship with nature and social relations.

What has already been said in general terms for the twenties — the investigation of experiences, the 'temporariness' in form and content of interpersonal relations, the emotional involvement in success and failure, the *Himmelhoch jauchzend, zum Tode betrübt* — all this applies equally strongly to marriage. The finding of a private common way of life is the basis for a togetherness which in later years may grow into community of spirit. The shaping of an environment for the next generation is also a joint creativity. The arrival of children, the caring for them and the concomitant intensification of responsibility are powerful experiences and give polish and colour to the first phase of marriage.

For the single man or woman, friendships with the opposite sex during this phase are generally fairly open, uncomplicated, comradely, carried along by the ups and downs of the sentient soul. Towards the end of the twenties and the beginning of the thirties, however, all this changes, with the objectification of the general attitude to life. However, this last also takes place in marriage, and differences in temperament, opinions and life-style may acquire a new emphasis. Whereas during the twenties differences of opinion could flare up and then be cancelled out by 'kiss and make up', they now assume a different character. On the one hand there is the idea that 'that's how things are, I shall have to adapt', on the other hand there may be a tendency to withdraw into work or hobby, resulting in unobserved but insidious alienation between the partners. Eroticism seems to lose its lustre, sex becomes a routine; something deeper must be created if the relationship is not to degenerate into an objectively convenient arrangement. This deeper element can only be the conscious will to separate the essential from the inessential in the relationship with the partner. This will is in itself sufficient to open the eyes to the partner's individuality. From there, a feeling of warm comradeship, of mutual trust, develops. Later it will become clear that this warm comradeship, arising in the sentient soul period, is the basis for an even deeper mutual closeness from which the relationship can develop into genuine love built on spiritual communion. At the same time the thirties can also create a practical basis for collaboration between man and wife and a flourishing of family culture (in, for example, family holidays as a phase of intimate assembly).

In the thirties the seeds are sown either for the marriage crisis in the forties or for a new relationship within the marriage during the same period, based on a spiritual meeting and relationship. The intellectual soul sees the pros and cons of other people very sharply; this may result in a cooling off or objectification of relationships, but such objectification may then lay the foundations necessary for the acceptance of the partner as he is, and may also lead to a growing bond with the leitmotiv which is gradually beginning to become audible and visible in the partner. Much depends on how the individual stands in relation to himself. The person who fails to accept himself with all his assets and defects, hiding self-confrontation behind the restless pursuit of career, success and status, will also be incapable of meeting his partner in his/her true personality. The marriage will then either begin to disintegrate or become the scenery for the 'external' play that is being performed. Such scenery may be useful, or it may be a distracting factor. In the latter case the individual will consider that it must be replaced by scenery better suited to the present act of the drama.

Much has already been said about the crisis of the forties. The person who in his thirties has not at least laid the foundations for a deeper encounter is likely to have a difficult time of it. This deeper encounter is tied up very closely with the image of man which, consciously or otherwise, each individual carries within himself. The person who is convinced that man's life is a purely biological affair awakens with a start to realize that the time is coming when the few pleasures which biology can provide are to be taken away from him. It is therefore understandable that in his longing for his own twenties the man is prone to develop a desire for a much younger partner. This is particularly true of the man – the woman is aware that she faces the menopause and its irrevocability, and many a late child is the fruit of an attempt to put off that evil day. As a 46-year-old woman put it when announcing her pregnancy: 'Just nipped through the door before the shop shut.'

The American psychoanalyst Edmund Bergler has written a book (*The Revolt of the Middle-Aged Man*) about the male menopause and its consequences in marriage. In the introduction to the Dutch edition (*Die illusie van de tweede jeugd*) Van Emde Boas says, 'Compared with the woman, the man in the change of life belongs to a forgotten group,' and, 'It may be said of the female menopause that in many cases it is a severe strain on the marriage. That of the man, however, is often a direct threat to it, for it is in this period that the middle-aged man often revolts against what he himself feels to be the chafing bonds of his existence.'

We do not have to agree with Bergler in his thesis that all neuroses (including this one, in other words) are based on what he calls 'mental masochism' in order to welcome this extremely useful book. His own discussion of the problem begins as follows: 'Man's middle-age revolt – the sudden discontent with everything (including marriage, professional duties, conventional pleasures) befalling men in their middle age – is the sad story of an emotional second adolescence, in which the words are of the cloak-and-dagger variety, the deeds inadequate, and the finale a predictable defeat. Inevitably, the revolt is abortive and leads to one of two consequences: acceptance, with good grace, of the rebel's individual and unchangeable (because self-created) fate—including the wife he will not divorce in spite of grandiose plans—or an even more tangled network of difficulties through which he plunges to find himself exactly where he began, but full of bitterness and reproaches.'

Bergler then goes on to describe in a series of chapters the endless and fruitless battles about futilities, where the main point is always that his partner refuses to let him go, and that he fails to be creative because of domestic circumstances. The chosen one who does understand him is, however, seldom promoted to the status of being his wife— divorce is no help when the situation has become a neurosis. The difficult part of this situation is that after *her* menopause the wife gains a new vitality (as described earlier), which gives her the illusion that she has become timeless, that she is now getting no older and that she is just as attractive as ever. At the same time the man in his dangerous years is living with the illusion of second youth. The wife is more capable of seeing clearly the foolishness of his behaviour, and is deeply offended by his reproaches. The husband wants to break out of the oppression to which he believes himself to be subjected; he sees no way out for an existence worthy of a human being.

It will be clear that this situation develops where each individually or both together can find no new spiritual content in their lives which could open up new dimensions and which gives precisely that feeling of having reached the point at which the leitmotiv becomes conscious and through which new aims in life fill the soul. The situation is resolved not by looking back at the biological past, but by finding a new task which will kindle new enthusiasm in a new horizon just becoming visible.

It is understandable that as a psychoanalyst Bergler should state categorically that it is impossible to escape the revolt of middle age 'because youth is not retrievable ... Everyone (at this age) must swallow the bitter pill and acknowledge that youth is lost ... Knowledge of the inevi-

table inner conflict, of the typical emergence of hypochon-
driacal complaints, of the transitory—and as far as end
effects go, harmless—character of the whole storm-in-a-
cocktail-shaker'—familiarity with this could help the wife
stand by her husband during this phase, just as earlier she
expected to be supported during her own menopause.
More severe cases can only be helped through psychoanalysis, according to Bergler. What I miss in his book is any
indication of the path to a new meaning to life and new
personal relations born of the spirit. A true therapy cannot,
therefore, consist of acquiescing to a biological involution,
but must be found in together seeking a new meaning to
life, from which, in turn, new encounters, including new
encounters between man and wife, become possible. It goes
without saying that the entire situation can also be directed
at the situation at work. Here too, it is always 'the others'
who stand in the way of the individual's own (illusory)
development. Here again, the man in this situation is
moving towards a tragic future, generally full of bitterness
at the failure of others to recognize his rightful claims to a
particular position. The difficulty here is that a genuine
therapy is usually rejected; the individual cannot and will
not face up to reality. Only a new encounter can bring help.

This new encounter in marriage is only possible if the
individual can in some manner or other see the personality
of his partner divorced from the instrument of the body. For
some this may be a religious vision, for others it may be
more of a philosophy, for yet others, perhaps, a deep-rooted
faith in the ego of his fellow men. Be that as it may, the
individual must be capable of becoming aware of the shape
of his partner's personality in order to be able to come to
know and love it. In general, this is easier for the woman
than for the man; the man experiences the *alter ego* through
the 'female' in himself, which plays a special role during the
forties.

From this relationship, which gradually reaches the stage

at which it may be termed love, there grows the faithfulness which will eventually extend beyond the death of the partner and which remains positive whatever happens to the partner. This relationship, which is born in the thirties during the development of the intellectual soul, must be tended with care so that it can reach maturity in the fifties. It is a love that is generous, not demanding. Marriage in old age can grow yet further in intensity. Where common spiritual or artistic interest has grown up, stimulating discussion is still possible in later years, but wordless communion in one another's knowledge can also give a deep sense of happiness. This is in bitter contrast to the predicament of those elderly couples whom one sees in the lounges of hotels, sitting facing each other in silence, until the one says to the other, 'Stop rubbing your nose like that,' to which the reply is, 'If I want to rub my nose I'll rub my nose,' after which the 'non-communal' silence is continued. Here the marriage has decayed until it has become a silent battle for the repeated preservation of some futile liberty, an uninterrupted wrestling-match in which the eternal repetition of the same futile reproaches has turned into trench warfare.

With the acquisition of insight into the personality of the partner, essentially *negative* aspects of their make-up, now seen from close range, become apparent. This other 'Gestalt' can be concentrated into an experience of the partner as a repulsive monster or at least as a caricature of the positive personality.

The wife of a writer, a highly educated and talented woman, once told me the following story (their marriage, incidentally, was seen by their many friends as a model of a happy marriage). Her husband had just finished a book and had then gone away on a long journey. She stayed at home with the children, taking upon herself the task of reading the proofs of the new book. One evening, deeply engrossed in this work and because of her careful reading strongly involved with its contents, she suddenly saw in her mind's eye an abhorrent being which awakened every grain of hate that was in her. A moment later it had disappeared, but the emotion of this 'encounter' lingered on, just as a vivid dream may occupy our thoughts for weeks afterwards. It became clear to her that in this abhorrent being she had seen a sort of personification of everything that was negative in her husband, the effect being heightened by his absence and at the same time by his spiritual presence in the book. In her sensible way she said to me: 'I suppose that was just one of the things I had to go through to be able to love him all the more.'

Not everyone will experience this process quite so clearly. For the kind of experience just related one must oneself be an artist, used to dealing intuitively with such contents. But on the threshold of consciousness we all go through it. We know the 'double' or shadow side of our loved one and it plagues us in greater and lesser irritations, which disrupts what consciously we wish to say or do. Indeed, we know our loved one's double better than our own, with which we only become familiar when we learn to observe the effect we have on others, and how good intentions are repeatedly misunderstood. Instead of seeking the fault in others, we must be capable of daring to see our own negative selves, if not as a *Gestalt* then at least as a sense (*Ahnung*) of a *Gestalt*.

In Wolfram von Eschenbach's *Parzival*, at the point where Parzival has been accepted by King Arthur as a Knight of the Round Table, a figure in the shape of Kundrie appears, terrible to behold, and cries out that Parzival has been unjustly honoured because he is under the curse of not having asked the question at the Castle of the Grail. Here Kundrie is the anima who is at the same time the double. That this is so becomes clear at the end of *Parzival*. When after all his trials Parzival eventually does become the Grail King, Kundrie comes to meet him, but now she has become a shining figure, absolved as she is of her task of presenting the negative side of things.

In the marriage crisis of the forties the failure to recognize one's own double, alongside the clear perception of the double of the partner, plays an important role. Because of my work I have, alas, become in a sense involved in many divorce problems. Long discussions with the two parties involved often left one with the impression that here were two people who were in themselves excellent people. But each saw only the double in the other and lost sight of the other's true individuality. Upon closer investigation it becomes clear that although these two people have spent many years together they have *not* been sharing their joys and sorrows, so that the atmosphere of reproach grew stronger than the deep joy which the knowledge of trust in another can bring. Unfortunately, when things have reached this stage it is rarely possible for the individual to open his eyes to the essential qualities of his partner; for that, the distance of many years is often necessary — and by then it is too late.

Thus marriage follows the human life path, and the success or failure of a marriage does indicate whether the individuals are capable of reaching maturity. Their marriage is the mirror of the partners' inner development towards maturity, and the marriage can only reach maturity if the partners in it continue to grow to become total personalities. This completeness of the individual's humanity may be the fruit of a long life, in which he may test his own development through the continuity of his bond with another individuality. The person who has never renounced the scapegoat psychology, and is unaware that true development begins with the acceptance of one's own 'being' for what it is, will never achieve true self-knowledge. It is this self-knowledge which, in turn, is the guide by which each individual may tread the path of life.

It would be wrong to conclude from the foregoing that

unmarried people have no chance of following the path of development; it is simply that here we have been considering marriage as such. I shall turn to individual development in a later chapter.

There is no doubt that tension can also arise because of a wide difference in ages. But the same situation can also *prevent* tension! Whoever makes the effort to see everything together will arrive at the conclusion that only the continued development of one's inner life can help to prevent becoming bogged down in interpersonal relations.

Tensions which arise through finding a different philosophy of life or a different religion are more difficult to bridge. A high level of tolerance is necessary here in order to permit one's partner the freedom which one takes for granted for oneself.

We have yet to consider modern family culture. The term has already been used in this chapter, and it is important that something more be said about it. In the days when the family was a social unit composed of several generations, the family culture could be maintained by a division of tasks and duties among those generations. Rejuvenation was brought about by new marriages with their new outlook on the problems of living in the world. Continuity was borne by the older generation, who were in a position to impart to their grandchildren something of their worldly wisdom. It was from this situation that the folk-tales were bred which were told by the grandmothers, and the peasant wisdom which the grandfathers would produce in pithy proverbs. In numerous biographies, both now and in the past, I have been struck by the vital role played by the subject's grandfather or grandmother in his own life. But it is a role which is on the decline.

A new family culture, then, will have to be created by conscious efforts on the part of the parents themselves, in this case principally by the woman. There are a number of preconditions that must be met before a satisfactory family culture can be developed. The first is this: the life of the family must be imbued with a rhythm. We all know that an infant needs a fixed pattern to his daily life. Through regularity in feeding, sleeping and playing, inner security is born in the child in his dependence. Later, when the child is passing through the toddler and school stage of his life, this rhythm must find a form peculiar to his own family. Certain eating habits, for example, must be developed — fixed moments during the day at which the child can count upon there being a place and time for his own life. Or the rule that before bed-time there is half an hour of quiet communion, with story-telling or reading aloud, with a review of the events of the day, and so on. The old folk-tales still have their everlasting value for the young child. For the older child, made-up stories are more important. Here there is also a role to be played by the father, even if it is only that on Sunday mornings he is willing to relate a new episode in a serial story of his own invention. From my own experience I remember a little game which we used to play with our eight-to-twelve-year-olds. The children were allowed to think up a title, and their father then had three minutes for reflection after which he had to tell a story about the subject set him. The game consisted in the reciprocal challenge of inventing a title which would leave the father at a loss for a story, and the enjoyment was then all the greater if he nevertheless succeeded. Such an exercise is important not only for the children. For the father in his thirties and forties, too, it is an eminently important experience. He will find himself thereby developing a power which will be of great help to him on his own path through life. Successful stories then become standard stories existing only within the family and constituting a firm foundation for a sense of belonging.

For parents, a child's desire to hear the same story repeated over and over again sometimes takes some getting used to. Sometimes the same story is called for month after month. The glee of anticipating the familiar high-spots of the story is enormous, and is paralleled by the wish always to return to the same place for the holidays so that acquaintance can be renewed with familiar places and faces.

In pre-puberty this pattern changes, making way for an increasing desire for hearing new stories or having new experiences. This is one of the phenomena of the incipient conquest of a wider world.

Alongside the daily and weekly rhythms (Sunday being different from the rest of the week), celebrations are an important feature of the child's life. Fixed ceremonials for birthdays and Christmas are especially important, particularly if the children join in by making the preparations for the festivities themselves. For it is in the preparation that the most essential element of such occasions lies – trying to imagine how the others will be surprised by a particular decoration or game.

The joy of anticipation is always greater than the joy of accomplishment; it is the former which is remembered later in a warm glow of nostalgia.

We live in a harsh and uncertain age. What we can give our children in the way of warmth and security can never be taken away from them, whatever the future may bring. In this, the discovery and establishment of a relationship with nature and art plays a major role. Going for walks and becoming acquainted with the wonders of nature, collecting stones, sea-shells or plants, learning to identify birds – all these are food for the soul, just as important as correct physical nutrition. One and all should seek in this way to build up a piece of family culture, each according to his powers and possibilities. And for the dry sticks among us, those with little imagination and love of nature, the discovery, together with the children, of new worlds in nature, music, drawing, painting and telling stories can bring about self-thawing and correction of our own experiences in childhood.

I venture to suggest that the future of western culture depends largely on whether a new family culture will be created on a wide scale.

Chapter Four

Basic Life Orientations

The young person going through the process of discovering himself has to struggle with the questions: Who am I? What do I want? What am I capable of? The first of these is the most profound; it is an existential question that returns throughout our lives in new dimensions. For the moment it is important to answer the questions: What am I capable of and what do I want? Many have tried to arrive at a classification of people with similar aptitudes, to class them in a typology. Jung, for example, puts forward his extrovert and introvert types, each subdivided into four other types: extrovert thinking type, emotional type, sentient type and intuitive type; introvert thinking type, emotional type, sentient type, and intuitive type — in all, eight types which, as it were, form a compass rose for orientation in the mind. For the choice of profession, too, attempts have been made to come to a typology. Using a large volume of material, Hollander distinguished between six types: the intellectual, the enterprising, the realistic, the social, the conventional, and the artistic, statistically derived from the mental preference for particular professions or occupations. From my own experience of 40 years of conversations with young people, I myself have arrived at six types and two modalities of them: the enquiring, the thoughtful, the organizing, the caring, the innovatory and the conserving or administrative types, with creative and non-creative modalities. The creative modality makes the basic attitude a creative art, the non-creative an aptitude. I have called these types the basic orientations.

Unlike Hollander, who develops his types on the basis of existing occupations, by the concept of 'basic orientation' I refer to what might be termed the key in which the composition of the biography is set. And just as the key by itself tells us nothing about the content of the composition set in it, nor about the tempo or the instrument, but about the 'mood' in which the composition will unfold itself, so the basic orientation tells us nothing about the content of the drama of life, nor about its tempo or instrumentation. It does, however, lend life a certain quality: *the basic orientation is an expression of the inherent nature of the mind itself.* The mind receives its leitmotiv from the world of the spirit, and its drives and desires from the world of the biological. But the soul, too, has a structure of its own, and this becomes recognizable and capable of investigation in the basic orientation. A person with an enquiring basic orientation will always have the urge to investigate things, whether he or she is a scientist, scholar, housewife or gardener.

Musical aptitude may be a question of heredity. Through the temperament it acquires an active or passive form; through the basic orientation the form acquires a certain quality. But it is the ego that determines whether music is to be the leitmotiv of this particular life or whether it will simply be a pleasant bonus. Only in the former case can the biography of a musician arise. Hereditary aptitude and temperament are clearly experienced in the mind as being instrumental, as being qualities that one can exploit or not. It is extremely difficult to distance oneself from one's own basic orientation in the life of the mind. Generally, this is only possible when one looks back on life at a later age. In adolescence, when our own leitmotiv has not become clearly apparent, the basic orientation often substitutes for it, becoming then the criterion for the choice of study and profession.

Essentially, every basic orientation is conceivable in every profession. A doctor, for example, can realize enquiring, thoughtful, organizing, caring, innovatory or administrative forms in his work. To which one he will feel attracted—the one in which he will probably perform best—depends on his mental structure, his basic orientation. However, if his leitmotiv has become conscious, he can also switch to another quality and develop another orientation than the predominant one. In that case, things will not happen by themselves, but he will be far more aware of the qualities he seeks to work with.

In the first half of life the basic orientations play a more determinant role than in the second half, after the forties. The basic orientation is, as we have seen, the quality, colour, key of the mind, *and will therefore have the greatest influence during the middle phase of life*. In adolescence, with the culturally determined need for a choice of study and/or profession, the basic orientation is highly significant in this choice. A choice which clearly contradicts the predominant basic attitude will lead to feelings of repulsion and insufficiency. Herein lies, in my view, an important cause of the singularly poor performance achieved by university studies, where the programmed courses of lectures and classes leave increasingly few opportunities for developing one's own style of studying.

I have used the term 'predominant basic orientation', and I shall have to elucidate it. The six or seven basic orientations are present in each and every one of us, but one of them, at least, predominates, imparting its colour to the first half of life up to and including the expansionary phase. For people with one clearly dominant basic orientation the problem is not difficult. In that case, the adolescent will feel a definite preference for a particular way of wanting to behave in life. But Hollander, too, has pointed out that for many people there is more than one possibility. For them, the choice is not so easy. They have a tendency to let first the one, then the other orientation of the soul prevail. For them, the choice of career—and for career advisers, advice—is particularly difficult.

It is my belief that in this case Rogers, with his non-directive conversations, has shown us a way of helping young people make their own final choice in the knowledge that they could have chosen something else. In the later stages of life that something else may be able to play a part in special circumstances, or as an activity besides the career. As such, unilateral basic orientations make for an initial easy choice but later result in the narrowing of possibilities. There is no space here to deal with the basic orientations in any more than a cursory fashion, but we may not leave them out entirely when considering the factors which influence the human life-path. It will be necessary to go into the problem in greater depth in a separate publication; for the moment, I shall content myself with describing the basic orientations and pointing to a number of mutually supportive and contradictory basic attitudes.

The enquiring type feels a need to investigate the way the world about him functions and how the relations between the phenomena of the world can be explained. At the same time the subject of his enquiry is of secondary importance; it may be language, matter, co-operation, manuring, or what have you. There are people, for example, who have devoted their whole lives to the study of the earthworm and know everything there is to know about that humble creature. The researchers of a clearly delineated field, be it a branch of chemistry or the structure of a beetle's jaws, run the risk of turning into 'little grey men' and going through life with blinkers. Anybody who has tried to run a research laboratory knows how difficult it is to knit his team of researchers into a cohesive whole. The creative researcher tends towards single-mindedness, the non-creative tends towards routine work and is prepared if necessary to listen to what others say.

The thoughtful type feels a need to order his world of ideas in systems and theories, generally in fairly broad categories. Aside from philosophers, who have made thinking the central theme of their lives, there are thinkers as well as researchers in every academic discipline or branch of scholarship. Many research workers are poor thinkers, feeling no affinity for putting existential questions or placing their partial knowledge in a greater epistemological whole. In my discussion of nativism I have drawn attention to the suspect simplifications exhibited by great researchers in biochemistry when they turn to philosophizing about the future of human nature. On the other hand, one-sided thinkers have difficulty in finding their connection with concrete humanity.

The thoughtful type reveals himself at an early age, and generally has a hard time of it at school because wherever he looks he finds inconsistencies and asks awkward questions. He regards the modern multiple choice examination as an insult to his intelligence, and is at a disadvantage because, unlike his more mediocre school-mates, he cannot slot into the thought patterns of the examiners and their 'one best way' philosophy. In his book *The Tyranny of Testing*, Benn Hoffman, with typical humour, discusses this problem at some length.

The organizing type is not hard to describe. For him, the world is there to be tackled, ordered and ruled. This type too becomes evident at an early age, at school and in the social life of children and young people. I have already described the early thirties as the organizational phase of life; and it is therefore understandable that it is during his early thirties that the organizing type goes through the peak of his life. The danger then, however, is that such people get bogged down in organizing things and find it difficult to make room in their lives for values other than those of practical functionality.

The organizing type is active to the point of aggression, and consciously or unconsciously seeks to acquire power over people and things. In our industrial society it is they who make up the core of 'hard' management and careerists. If this basic orientation is tempered by one of the other basic orientations (which happily is often the case), the urge to organize assumes a more amicable character. Organization can be directed to research, to thinking itself, to caring for others, to innovation or to management.

The caring type feels a need to tend to everything living, to feed it, care for it, make it flourish. This attitude is the foundation of education and nursing, and plays a role in agriculture, horticulture and animal husbandry. In social life he creates an environment in which others can develop and flourish without himself moving into the foreground. Without the caring basic orientation there would be no conviviality and no sense of security in life. It is extremely important that children be able to grow up in surroundings in which the caring orientation prevails. An overactive mother who always turns out to have organized everything beforehand continually creates feelings of menace and insufficiency in growing children.

The innovatory basic orientation has many facets. It implies a desire to change and improve that which already exists. In life, this can manifest itself in the desire to cure people of illness and disease, or in the revolutionary who is prepared to destroy society in the hope that a better one will arise from the ashes. By saying that, we have already established that there are many possible facets to the innovatory orientation. Every great innovator in education, science, religion or society has had these basic tendencies in himself. Often they have given their lives for their inner convictions; they are what Neumann calls 'the heretics of the inner voice'. They are destined always to be persecuted, yet they will never relinquish their urge for innovation. In their choice of career they are prepared to seek new, as yet unexisting professions, which they then create for themselves. Being the first in a new profession or career gives them the freedom which they need in order to be able to live.

In less extreme cases they go through life as non-conformists. In the medical profession there is a clear distinction between those with a scientific interest and researchers on the one hand and those who are primarily concerned with healing, such as many general practitioners. For them the physically sick person constitutes an intolerable situation, so that they continue their search for ways of curing him.

The conserving or administrative basic orientation, unlike the foregoing, is a desire to maintain that which already exists, to record it, reproduce it, control it and possibly even evaluate it. It is an attitude often found in bookkeepers, librarians and the like, including journalists and diplomats. The good journalist presents the news as objectively and in as well ordered a fashion as possible, the diplomat represents his government and not his own opinions. It is important to note that this orientation must not be seen as something negative. Without the administration and conserving of what we already have, development can have no foundation upon which to proceed. An ordered and accessible past is the basis of the present and the starting-point for the future.

It is difficult to see *the creative basic orientation* as something which manifests itself as such except, perhaps, in artists. The creative basic orientation pervades the six others, calling them to life and activity. The creative investigator, the creative thinker, organizer, carer, innovator, administrator lets his own personal motivation shine through the basic attitude and makes it something personal, so that only now his own biography becomes a real biography and not a passive fate. *In creativity the spirit becomes visible in the mind.*

The basic orientations are the element most peculiar to the structure of the mind. The ego has to deal with these basic orientations as with the quality of the instrument which it must play and use. The basic orientation of the mind is the equivalent of the constitution for the biological person. The ego has also to reckon with a constitution as with a given quantity, and the person is body *and* psyche *and* spirit; his freedom is thereby limited but continues nevertheless to exist in the attitude which the ego adopts towards this limitation. We might also say: the ego retains the freedom to choose how it uses its constitution and basic orientation, how it wishes to put them to work in the service of its aims.

Adler has already pointed to the possibility of compensating for physical inadequacy; the same applies to the basic orientations of the mind. And this reveals itself in attitudes to life and the world, where the ego makes its own choice and, in later life, can bring a weak basic orientation to maturity.

Where people grow up in a particular religion or philosophy, too, if one perseveres with it one will again have to win it for oneself and prove it, for 'paper' adherents of a religion or philosophy are no good to anyone.

It is also possible to leave the religion or philosophy of one's youth in order as a mature person to make one's own choice. That this is an existential ego-choice is clear from the dangers that people are prepared to face where a personal choice is culturally or politically potentially fatal. Again and again we see that many prefer to sacrifice biological life rather than deny the spirit.

Chapter Five

Career Prospects and Personnel Policy

The young person's expectation for his working life, his career prospects, vary widely from person to person.

Young working people, whether or not they have undergone some sort of training, used to be the first to be faced by the necessity of choosing their occupations and training. The future prospects for 16-year-old boys and girls in a life in the lowest echelons of the industrial hierarchy, with no prospect of ever being able to break free from that hierarchy, did not usually become apparent to them until later. This has now changed. Young working people have now built up an active organization to promote their own interests which is doing admirable work. The technical training of the 1950s, often well-intentioned but not capable of changing anything in the situation, has gone through a process of development over the years and has reluctantly made the move towards making contact with further vocational training in the apprentice system. This is not the place to discuss the unprofitable contradictions between these two forms of education. In participatory education, as proposed by the Lievegoed Commission in Holland and adopted by the Dutch Government, the foundations have been laid for a fruitful amalgamation of both possibilities of development.

The Lievegoed Commission's report was based on the assumption that every individual has a right to education until the age of 18, and, moreover, that the education which he receives must be capable of meeting the needs and accommodating the personality structure and hopes for the future of a major proportion of young people in general. On the road towards achieving this aim, a road now being travelled, albeit with some difficulty, interim solutions are needed which will be able to accumulate teaching experience for a new movement in education. The shining example was the Hibernia School at Wanne-Eickel in Germany, which has had considerable influence on the ideas of the *Gesamtschule* in Germany. Here, a complete 'Free School' or 'Waldorf School' with a course lasting 12 years was coupled with a course of training for a trade in which all pupils took part. The result of this fusion was secondary education leading to craft diplomas without closing off the possibility of taking a school-leaving examination which itself might lead to higher education. Present experiments in Holland involving the so-called Middle School have yet to prove whether this form of education is suitable for application on a wider scale.

Although the step-by-step lengthening of the period of compulsory schooling means that young people enter the adult production world at a later age than was previously the case, without the possibility of an *éducation permanente* their future is more or less predetermined when they leave school. After a period in which they earn the lower rates paid to young people they move into the adult pay scales which offer them no future because the top is rapidly reached and a 'career' is only possible after specialization or a period in a post in minor management. Whichever path one chooses, a limited number of places is available. Later in this chapter we shall see an example of what industry can do in this quarter. Things are different for those able to go through further intellectual training. The higher forms of secondary education (grammar schools and the like) are the final stage here, and at the same time they are the starting-blocks for further academic education.

We now find ourselves faced by a particular problem. As part of the effort to provide individually tailored education for one and all, a selection of subjects can *and must* be made, either in the middle of puberty or during the transition from puberty to early adolescence. The pupil himself is not yet sufficiently mature to make a responsible choice, so that the so-called choice which *is* made is based on his school results so far. And from that moment on the social bond of the class is broken — each individual goes his own way from one subject room to another. Anybody who has spent much time talking to young people in this situation knows that here again social upbringing has been sacrificed to intellectual education. Far more serious, however, is the fact that very many young people have a sense of having been trapped by the decision taken in the past. The world is beginning to open itself to them, but the number of doors through which they may pass proves to be small. Supplementary examinations in a number of subjects are an emergency solution of which little practical use can be made. What is important is that adolescents should be able to develop the widest possible horizons on the structure of society, the images of professions, opportunities for training, and matters relating to philosophies and outlooks on the world. The chosen course of education leads finally to a job which for many is still invisible. Careers information is a vital necessity.

The young person embarking in his twenties upon a job in a factory or an office or in one of the service industries still has before him the time of searching for and experiencing his own orientation in life. He ought to be able to find or create something of the journeyman period. Leaving a work situation as soon as one has learnt all there is to be learnt ought to be the norm. Too many people are tied to one particular sort of work in which they have long since acquired all the necessary skills, unless their employer has been sensible enough to see to it that they can go through a number of different learning situations. During the twenties the main thing is to have experienced as many different situations as possible and to have accepted and met various challenges. This phase can be concluded at about 28, when the individual has accumulated sufficient experience to be able to oversee the beginning of a career within his chosen field.

Because of the increased length of the period of study, those who go on to university or college after leaving school have to go through an artificially prolonged dependent adolescent phase. The fact that they find themselves in responsible professional positions, with all the challenges, hopes and fears which go with them, at a later age than those who go straight from school into a job means that they are missing something which can never be made good with the same intensity of experience that is possible only in the phase of *Himmelhoch jauchzend – zum Tode betrübt*.

During the late Middle Ages people were apprenticed to a master while still in puberty. Being obliged to live in the master's house, and being treated as one of the family, the apprentice adopted the style of life and professional ethic without even noticing it. Later, at about 20, the years of wandering as a journeyman began, when the apprentice travelled about the country working for different masters from whom he learnt different aspects of his chosen trade. Half-way through his thirties he was then able to take his master's test and set himself up in business. The master was only allowed to take on apprentices if he was married, for it was in the master's family that the apprentice gained his experience. In this whole system there was still an instinctive understanding of the essentials of the various phases of life. Today we all have to design our own careers using our own experiences and insights as the building-blocks. Good personnel policy could create the right environment for this. In any case, to make someone do the same work for 10 years at a stretch during this phase of life is the worst conceivable approach.

The thirties are the years of hard work, of organization and continuity and of persevering in one's chosen field. The individual has to prove that he can hold his own. The ups and downs of this phase can be regarded in a more sober light. If there is any time of life when it is possible, this is the time for fighting for insights and results. From this there grows increasing assurance, including certainty about what the individual is incapable of and what he must give up trying to achieve. The working man in the second half of his thirties is at the peak of his performance capability in the quantitative sense. He knows his job, and he knows what he is worth and what he wants to achieve.

The forties. As we have already seen, there comes a breach in this assurance at the approach to and the crossing of the frontier into the fortieth year. Doubt about the absolute value of continuing along the path upon which one has embarked, alongside a fear of reduced performance, leads to a demand for new values. This is the moment for external training on a course or in a working-group, for meeting others with the same problems in other jobs, for becoming acquainted with new methods and, above all, new values and insights. In short, a broadening of horizons is urgently required. Within this broadened horizon, in which objectives may now be seen which were previously invisible, the individual must now re-evaluate his position and set a new course. The questions which have to be answered are: What do I want? Am I all right where I am? Have I got to change my job? What must I change in myself? What have I got to do *differently*?

The answers to these questions determine the final continued growth and the fulfilment of the promise of life. These years will decide the issue once and for all: Can I develop further to management level? If so, can I do it where I am, or must I go and do something completely different? If new tasks have been found by the end of the forties, either within the same or in a different job, this has a rejuvenating effect on the person concerned. The effects of such rejuvenation can be felt in the physical side of life as well, and bring about new vigour during the fifties. If that fails, symptoms of ageing soon develop, including raised blood pressure, premature greying and a shrunken appearance.

The fifties. Thus the fifties become a choice between the 'eminent leader' and the 'frustrated tyrant'. A man may blame life, his job or his family for his becoming a frustrated tyrant, but he has himself 'arranged' it; he has spent decades working hard to achieve it. It is the direct consequence of a *choice of life*!

But even then, all is not lost. A person who detects in himself the symptoms of frustration during this phase of life, and discovers a tendency in himself to take it out on others in a form of tyranny, can still catch up with what he ought to have done during his forties. In my practice I have seen heroic examples of this. True, a bit of a push from outside was always necessary, sometimes in the form of a change of job imposed from above, but I know from experience that a single developmental therapeutic talk can bring about a revolution.

'Eminent leaders', at all levels from foreman to managing director, breed other eminent leaders around them; unfortunately, however, frustrated tyrants breed frustrated tyrants. And for this reason alone everything must be done to restart a developmental process even at this late stage. The American expression 'keep the man on the move' is particularly appropriate in the forties and for the transition from the forties to the fifties.

One aid which is useful for putting oneself back on the road to development is the exercise of positive thinking. Here a very simple expedient can be of assistance. Take a decent-sized exercise-book and write in it, every evening, one positive experience of the day. Just a few lines will suffice, such as: when I left the house today the sun was shining through the leaves of the chestnut on the corner; or, when I went into the meeting X looked up with a pleased expression. If you keep this up for a few months you will come to realize how much there is to be glad about in every day.

A second aid is the exercise of equanimity, saying to yourself 'who cares?' or 'so what?' Make a note of how often you do *not* lose your temper in spite of the odds.

The third is 'imposing upon yourself' an intense interest in the development of younger people working with you. Consider what Jones was capable of a year ago and what he has learnt in the meantime; give him a bit of praise every now and then, or give him a bit of fatherly advice. Try generally to lend a hand to help your younger colleagues in their development.

Then the sixties are upon us. Don't get out too late! Take advantage of the possibilities of shorter working hours or early retirement; prepare something new to do, bearing in mind that the essential thing is that what you have learnt so far in your life must be allowed to be exploited to the full. And once you have reached retirement age, make sure that you have some new creative activity which you can begin at once. Learn to paint, build a boat, go to evening classes or learn all you can about a new country, its culture, art, language, and people. Whatever it is, *do something new*! At the same time, there will be all sorts of more general social activities which you can now join in at your own speed. See to it that you stay fresh mentally, positive, interested, a blessing to all about you. In the years that remain you will then be able to enjoy the fruits of life.

Personnel policy

A healthy personnel policy embraces staff administration and care, human relations, and, at its core, personnel development. It is to the last of these that I now wish to turn my attention. Anybody who engages young people below the age of 20 knows that he is accepting into the working community a group which is difficult to integrate. This is difficult because it is no simple matter to guarantee continuity of work when people are away for two days in the week for sandwich courses and other vocational training. Theoretically, of course, everything is capable of organization, but for certain sorts of work for which a certain measure of practice is necessary this can give rise to special problems. The reverse side of the coin of the transition to partially compulsory education is that there is considerable unemployment among young people. The commission which paved the way for 'partial education' in the Netherlands was aware of this and proposed its gradual introduction at specified centres and planned expansion of the scheme over a period of between five and ten years.

For political reasons, however, the change had to be made at once and in its entirety—and neither partial education nor the labour market was prepared. The bitter fruits of political haste are now being tasted by jobless young people themselves. In the transitional stage, and in an unfavourable economic climate and a naturally already high turnover among working girls, the problem is not susceptible of solution by the personnel policy of a single industrial concern.

The situation is different for those aged over 20, who are part of the permanent work-force. For them, it is possible to create an efficient system of career guidance. For a large company and certain categories of young people with some training behind them, the NPI (Netherlands Pedagogical Institute) designed such a plan. Every young worker of 20 (many had come straight from national service) was invited to a personal discussion in which he was given the choice of either staying where he was, with good pay but few future prospects, or joining the group undergoing differentiated training. This was so arranged that those taking part were moved every 18 months or so to a different part of the firm to do a different sort of job. For each worker there was a personal card on which a record was kept of how well or badly he had assimilated the new training and what sort of opportunities he had had and utilized for social contact. When they reached the age of about 24 they were invited to a second discussion. The choice was again between staying in the fields now familiar to them or being trained even further, now for various possible specialities. Those who chose the latter course were taught the circumstances and requirements of a number of specialized branches of the business, such as administrative work in the stockroom and in the planning department. This took about six months. In a final discussion they were then asked if they wanted to carry on in one of these specialities or whether they wanted to go into management. In the latter case they had to go through several more periods of practical training so that they would later be familiar with all the different sections and branches of the company with which a manager would have to deal. During these periods of training they would be given the post of assistant manager until such time as a managerial position came free. The system worked well. The only complaint was that occasionally so many assistant managers were needed that they had already been appointed before they had gone through all the different parts of the company. But that kind of situation is bound to the particular environment and may be quite different in another place or time.

For the young workers the position was clear: 'If I want, I can get on; if I don't, then I have only myself to blame if things go wrong.' A certain amount of natural selection also took place, of course, to sort out those who were more technically minded (the specialists) and those more interested in social relations (the managers). From the assessments made of each individual during the entire eight years of training (assessments to which he had access, incidentally) there was also a distinct feedback effect by means of which they could make their own judgement of their performance. In my discussion of this phase of life I have already pointed out how important this is during the twenties, when self-assessment has to be based on judgements passed by the outside world. The same is possible, of course, for those pursuing careers in administration.

Smaller companies which occasionally take on younger people of a particular category can nevertheless make use of this example to ensure the maximum spread of experience. In smaller organizations, individual functions are never so clearly delineated and formalized as in larger ones. There the 'journeyman' phase can be less formal and more personal, by allotting each younger person to the mentorship of an older and more experienced man who is charged with teaching him every facet of the job.

To make continued development possible in even later stages it is important that the personnel department work together with delegations from the work-force in order to establish the professional requirements for existing posts and to decide on the training and periods of practical experience necessary before an individual may be employed at a particular level in the organization. This, coupled with a quantitative assessment of the requirements of the various functions, gives both personnel department and worker a realistic idea of the training obligations for particular jobs and for the chances of being employed at particular levels. From there, everyone can draw his own conclusions and make his own plans.

For some years there was a general feeling that everything ought to be possible—that everyone ought to have the opportunity of receiving secondary education, that everyone ought to be allowed to go to university, and that everyone ought to be allowed to have a job at the level which he wishes to attain. The consequence of this illusory situation may now be seen as follows. The disease will have to run its course; everyone will have to learn that the time and the culture in which he lives are part of his biography. And every culture and every time has positive and negative features and a limit to its possibilities. The question is a simple one of how to deal with these factors and limitations.

For young people who enter the labour market at a later stage because they have been through training college or university, this phase of gaining experience in changing circumstances and in varying work is somewhat different. If an organization has an annual intake of ex-polytechnic students aged about 23, rotation can again take place in a number of departments. The time each individual spends in each department must be long enough for it to be more than just 'sightseeing'—say two years. Here again, there is a period of training and a period of real responsibility.

At the beginning of the thirties the choice has to be made yet again—either the individual goes to a particular department to have further training as a specialist or he turns to general management, perhaps as the assistant to the department manager. The one preference is for more technical and scientific work, the other is for the organizational side and for leading people.

Thus the organization has a core of motivated people aged about 35, each of whom has been able to find his own way in his own individual line of life. Where in a given instance a particular line cannot be followed within the organization, it is in the interests of both the organization and the individual that he move to another organization where it *can* be followed. Here the interests of company and employee are congruent.

No organization profits from having dissatisfied workers. No worker profits from work which is contrary to his biographical line. In other words, a measure of labour mobility is necessary which was until quite recently far from being the norm in Europe. For example, the man who 10 years ago in his mid-thirties applied for a job when he already had four previous jobs behind him was looked at askance. In America, by contrast, the same response could be expected by a man of the same age who had had only one previous job. Clearly, he had little initiative or desire to improve himself. Greater mobility on the labour market is something that should be furthered at all costs.

When a child is born, we know that it is not destined for everlasting life; one day it will die and make way for others who have been born. Organizations, on the other hand, are expected to last for ever. They may be born, but they are not supposed to die; that would be a disgrace. But human organizations, like every other form of life, have their own life-span. If that has come to an end but they are still kept alive, they become fossilized, their structures petrified. Either new, young initiatives must replace them, or they must be rejuvenated by a new generation arising from within to such an extent that they are practically born again. Our universities, for example, suffer from such fossilization effects, and it is a good thing that every now and then a thorough renovation should take place—renovations, of course, that must first prove their worth.

For anybody with an eye to it, it will have become clear that the organizations which men create go through phases of life similar to those of their creators. It is quite easy, for example, to see the teething, puberty and young adulthood of organizations. But this really requires separate study. An initial attempt at unravelling this problem may be found in my book *The Developing Organization*.

One special aspect of personnel policy is keeping a close watch on employees (at all levels) who are approaching the age of 40. To counteract their tendency to dig themselves in in one particular kind of work which gives them a sense of security, it becomes necessary to ask the following questions. Do they reject any thought of related or quite different jobs? Do they feel that they are absolutely indispensable? Do they, indeed, organize their work so that they *are* indispensable? Do young hopefuls regularly make their appearance from the department or area of those responsible and, helped by them to realize their ambition, go on to higher things and pass them by? Or do they keep all energetic youngsters under their thumb, frightened that they are a threat to their own positions?

All these questions have to be answered and discussed with those concerned. By half-way through the forties it should be apparent who is going to develop further to a higher level of adulthood, maturity and leadership and who will not be able to manage it without help. Not everybody has to make it to the top, but at all levels the organization needs people who are not on the way to becoming frustrated tyrants — be they managers, hospital matrons, bookkeepers or administrators. Petty tyrants in their fifties are a severe liability to any organization and the cause of much pain to their unfortunate colleagues and subordinates. It is here that we can see whether the personnel department concerns itself merely with administrative and organizational work or whether it feels that part of its job is to tackle some development therapy.

In some cases assistance from outside can be of some use. An outsider poses no threat to one's position within the company and can say things that a colleague cannot.

Finally, personnel policy should also be concerned with preparing people for retirement, activating external social responsibility in district, school or social work.

Personnel *policy* must be represented right at the top of the organization; its implementation may be left to specialists, but its style and aims must be the responsibility of senior management. In the end, it is its personnel policy that determines the well-being of the organization itself.

Chapter Six

Images of Man, Biography and Psychotherapy

1. Modern Images of Man

After the brief introduction in 'Surveying the terrain', I want in this chapter to discuss the images of man that underly the various streams of thought in psychology, since in the foregoing treatment of the inner life path we looked at them from the viewpoint of personalism. Had I chosen a different standpoint, the general picture might have looked quite different. The reader has a right to know what those other possible standpoints are and which fields of knowledge can be explored from each one.

To begin with, we may say that different schools of thought operate with different images or models of man. In essence, there are four possible views. *First*, the technical-mechanistic and physical-chemical model. This is also known as the medical model. *Second*, the biological model, the most important aspect of which is the heredity model, or nativism. *Third*, the psychological model, the most important schools of thought here being behaviourism and empiricism. A variant of this is the sociological model, which considers that man is shaped exclusively by his social class. *Fourth*, the personalistic model, divided into: (a) pseudo-personalism, the idea that personality arises from an interaction between heredity and experience; and (b) true personalism, the idea that there is an authentic 'third force' besides heredity and upbringing. This third force is then referred to as the personality, the individuality, the higher ego, or the self, depending on the author. The higher ego, or whatever one likes to call it, is then a spiritual *Gestalt* in a spiritual reality.

Although each of these schools regards its own choice as the only scientific one, it will be clear to anyone capable of seeing more than one point of view or wishing to consider various different models that each view has developed or is developing its own scientific method, that each viewpoint allows certain questions and can provide certain answers within the limitations imposed by the chosen model and scientific method.

With a psychological or personalistic model it is not possible to solve physical-chemical problems; a biological model cannot be used to solve psychological or personalistic problems. In other words, each model produces a *reduced image of man*. In this connection we speak of biologism, psychologism and sociologism. Marxism and historical materialism assume a sociologistic image of man; behaviourism assumes a psychologistic image of man.

These images may be found alongside each other in different psychological schools, but it is also possible to point to fluctuations of fashion in the choice of image as the basis for what one believes. At the turn of the century, for example, *biological nativism* was 'the' standpoint of the scientific and then modern individual. The entire life path was determined by coincidence in the mixing up of heredity factors, and at the end of life everything came to an end.

During the 1920s *behaviourism* came to the fore. Heredity played hardly any role at all; man was conditioned in his behaviour by his upbringing and culture. Watson would say: 'Give me a certain number of healthy, well-formed babies, and I will make of each of them what you want me to.'

Empiricism found favour chiefly in America, where it became the basic tenet behind a wave of pedagogic enthusiasm, since by better conditioned upbringing a better world could be created!

Personalism in its present form did not appear on the scene until the 1930s. After the Second World War a somewhat vague pseudo-personalism became the basis of the reshaping of education, which was no longer supposed to be a process of conditioning or training but had to lay the foundations for self-discovery, self-development and self-realization. The main thing was to arouse the creativity of the individual. Later the same aims were imposed on adult education and social work.

At the same time there are fanatical adherents of nativism and empiricism in education, busily clearing away all the ethical prattle about the dignity of the personality. The watchword is sometimes *selection*, sometimes *programmed instruction*, and people are even prepared to shake hands on it — if only the 'person' keeps out of it. This abhorrence for the person in man can sometimes manifest itself in unexpected places. An article by the Dutch biologist D. Hillenius in which he reviews Skinner's book *Beyond Freedom and Dignity* begins with the following paragraph: 'I must say that *Beyond Freedom and Dignity* makes good reading, especially at the beginning, *for anyone who is regularly irritated* by the *preaching* about the *deep motives* of the human soul, about the *unique*, the *autonomous*, the *self-awareness*, and the *liberty* of man.' (Author's italics.)

This, then, is a discussion by a genuine nativist of a book by the most outspoken representative of empiricism. Not surprisingly, then, Hillenius soon loses interest, since Skinner says not a word about heredity. But this criticism remains within scholarly limits. More peculiar is the denigrating tone and the irritation which are displayed as soon as personalism is mentioned. Could it be that this irritation indicates a desire forcibly to silence something within the reviewer himself?

The technical-mechanistic model
The technical-mechanistic model had a number of supporters during the last century and at the beginning of this. Man was seen as a conglomeration of a number of

machines. In the medical model, the image of the heart as a pumping-station is still popular.

Alongside the technical-mechanistic model there developed a physical-chemical model in which life and the total man is seen as a great chain of chemical reactions which are simply there, in 'life', and on the basis of which everything is capable of being explained. A renaissance of the physical-chemical model took place half-way through the twentieth century in biogenetics. I shall have more to say about this when discussing the biological model of nativism.

Nativism

In modern nativism we have a reduced image of man in which man is a biological object — completely programmed by the genetic code, or, in popular terms, by heredity. In other words, man is what is termed 'endosomatic', or determined from the inside. From this we may deduce that nativism has no interest in the 'spiritual' biography of man. For nativists there are only three phases: youthful growth, adult equilibrium, and decline or involution. All other manifestations of the human life path must be explained in terms of these three stages. At the same time, only during the phase of youthful growth is 'development' (of a given 'envelopment') possible.

The history of nativism is as old as that of mankind. On the one hand, breeding domestic animals was an ancient industry and breeders had an intuitive knowledge of the working of heredity. On the other hand the heredity of caste, royalty, nobility, and later of profession, was the basis of the social order in human communities. Heredity was the rock upon which feudal society was founded. It bestowed rights and privileges, but also demanded duties and obligations. God had created men in ranks and classes — man was born to be master or servant. To break out of this pattern was to betray one's class and deserve death.

A new nativism arose during the nineteenth century in

the course of the search for a theory of human evolution. Names such as Darwin and Haeckel are sufficient indication of the direction taken by this school.

In the twentieth century this theory of the descent of man was taken a step further in the psychoanalysis of Freud, who declared that all culture was no more than a superstructure, a sublimation of man's animal drives, which controlled everything. And these drives were determined by heredity. At the same time, behaviour was determined to a considerable degree by the individual's experience of life after birth. But under this accommodated behaviour lurks animal man, with but one drive—the *libido sexualis*.

A recent attempt to indoctrinate the public with a primitive Darwinism-nativism could be seen in the film *Ape and Super-Ape* (original Dutch title *Bij de beesten af*) by Bert Haanstra, who informs us that the film was made under the guidance of biologists and scientists. An extreme form of Darwinism was also brought to the public's attention in Desmond Morris's best-seller *The Naked Ape*.

In the middle of the twentieth century a new branch of nativism became apparent: biogenetics. It is the biogeneticists who have researched the chemistry of the bearers of heredity, the genes, and built the model of the giant spirally structured molecule DNA. Like the punched tape which feeds a computer, this molecule carries the programming of the genetic code. Man had scarcely wrested himself from the grip of the ecclesiastical doctrine of predestination before the biological doctrine of predestination appeared to take its place.

Thus nativism has gone through the development from ancient social institution to hyper-modern scientific law. The two have one thing in common: man is determined by his birth—individual liberty is nothing but a façade.

As long as the biogenetic nativists remain exclusively practitioners of pure science, their so explicitly formulated axiomatic choice is legitimate. By limiting themselves to aspects of biological heredity they delineate their terrain, pose certain questions and receive answers which, in a context limited by the nature of the questions, become increasingly accurate. But as soon as they begin to leave the field of pure research and start trying to improve mankind by manipulating its genetic material, matters take on a different aspect. The biogeneticist has become a bio-technologist, meddling with *our* life. And they have far-reaching plans; their ideal is a world controlled and run by biochemists. This ideal was made known to the world at a symposium held in London in 1962, attended by all the big names in biochemistry including a fair sprinkling of Nobel Prize-winners. The manipulation of genetic elements for the purpose of creating useful variants on the 'human species' was considered not only feasible in principle but also attainable within 20 years (see *Man and His Future*, London 1963, and elsewhere). This would mean the bringing in of a new era of salvation for mankind.

The extreme nativists attempt to find an endo-somatic solution to *every* social problem. Nativist moderates are also interested in the extra-genetic so-called plasmatic heredity, about which more becomes known every year and which deals with the extra influence of the cell plasma of the egg cell on heredity.

In his critique of radical biotechnologists the Basle zoologist Adolf Portmann says: 'For the radical biotechnologist the insect state is a barely admitted wish-dream for the social life of man.' He also points to the dangers when the 'improvement techniques' get into the hands of power groups or doctrinaire politicians. And apart from that, published information about extra-genetic plasmatic heredity has made him suspicious of pronouncements made by geneticists.

Moderate nativists find themselves beginning to consider the problems of programme and environment. Is genetic coding really necessary? In other words, does it prescribe not only the physical forms but also the entire character during an entire life, or is the genetic code one of the factors in development? Does it create possibilities which are then exploited or not by the environment (by which I mean the biological and embryonal environment)?

The standpoint of nativism implies that we have to search in a certain direction to find the solution to educational problems in particular. Education will be governed by an annually more accurate *selection process*, usually innocently referred to in modern teaching circles as 'testing'. Only those who have come through a whole series of selection procedures and have been able to give precise responses to demands predetermined by educational technologists will acquire the right to the highest forms of education created for the super-intelligent. In France this system has long been popular, and has indeed led to the creation of the myth of the 'superschools', the Écoles Supérieures Polytechniques and the Hautes Écoles d'Administration. It is conspicuous that the pupils at these schools include a large proportion who are the children of past pupils. But surely that proves yet again that high intelligence is hereditary?

Others talk of a closed shop, open only to a small circle who play into each other's hands.

By way of objective testing for all classes, education in the Netherlands is being driven towards a continuous selection procedure in which the standards set by the testers are conclusive for all children, regardless of their personality structure. In typically English fashion a reaction has come to the tendency towards directing children to their allotted level by means of continuous selection. In Benn Hoffman's book *The Tyranny of Testing*, testing itself is criticized with irony and put in its true perspective. For the so-called objective results of school tests are far from equivalent for children with different personalities. The more intelligent children, in particular, and those inclined to reflection before response, are at a clear disadvantage as compared with those of moderate intelligence when it comes to multiple choice questions.

The book *Meritocracy* deals with the world of 2056 in a sort of science fiction story in which a society is described which is founded entirely on intelligence performance determined by tests conducted throughout the subjects' lifetimes. What emerges is that in that sort of society virtually all knowledge is determined by standards stemming from the past or set by testers. One and all have to pass through the same yoke. In the book, a revolt eventually breaks out among people wishing to set their own standards.

But all this does not answer the question of what is and what is not determined by heredity.

Only potential factors can be hereditary — dispositions to be able to learn certain things. Chorus lists the following hereditary factors: physical constitution, the functioning of the senses, the functioning of memory, certain elements of attention and interest, the type of intelligence, the addressability of the emotions, and the speed of development. These are all very general characteristics which still leave a great deal of freedom in the way in which they are used. In general terms we may say that in his biological make-up man is provided with a very wide range of possibilities. In every culture, demands are made on only a small proportion of these, while the rest are left unexploited. Like a plant, man possesses an immense number of 'sleeping eyes' which develop only under extreme circumstances (in a concentration camp, for example), *or* when the individual concerned, the ego, *decides* that they should be developed as part of the process of realizing his aims in life.

The empiricists are right in so far as they claim that far more can be developed than actually is developed by the coincidental history of life. Objections to empiricism only arise when development is made synonymous with conditioning or training.

The ego can achieve far more than the individual supposes on the superficial plane. In every human being there are slumbering powers which he is capable of bringing to fruition.

The choice of nativism determines the direction to be taken in the search for solutions to a series of problems. As I have already said, for schools this means continuous selection from class to class. For the choice of a career, it means the key-and-lock theory. The young person or applicant for a job is the key. The shape of the key may be determined by a large number of tests. If, then, we have the data on the various career openings, or keyholes, we can look for a lock which fits the key. Once it has been found, our problems are over. It is merely a matter of having the right man in the right place, a square peg in a square hole.

Nativists point to the influence of inherited aptitudes on the impression which the individual makes on his fellow beings. As regards the psychological character, certain dispositions are imprinted by heredity. Yet there are so many potential human capacities that only a small proportion of them are called upon by the culture and the environment in which the individual lives. (Consider, for example, our school systems with their national or state examinations.)

However, in man a psychic process of *Einverseelung* takes place, that is, a continuous active absorption of new contents *which help to shape* the person. (Chorus, *Ontw. psychol.*, p. 72.) 'Only instrumental, purely formal functions are hereditary. Furthermore, learning can only take place when the individual has reached a certain level of maturity: despite the many developments in the psychic and personality spheres, a certain hereditary ground-structure continues to exist throughout life. On this foundation many different sorts of constructions may be built, partially demolished and rebuilt.'

Empiricism and behaviourism

Empiricism and behaviourism seek their point of application in exo-somatic solutions, in influences by the environment *after* birth, in the upbringing and the conditioning of man's behaviour by his culture.

Empiricism has successfully pointed out the weak points in nativism. The most important criticism is biological; empiricists stress that man is a mammal which, unlike other mammals, is born with a paucity of instinct. To put it in scientific terms, man is a prematurely born, nidifugous animal. He has the open senses of the nidifugous bird but also the helplessness of the nidicolous. Here too, man is an exception in the animal world. Heredity may determine the colour of skin and hair, the overall shape and constitution, but as a mammal man is born too early. His embryonic period is cut short; his sensory paths are not yet myelinized. What a calf can do, as a fellow nidifugous animal – stand, walk, and find its way to its mother – the human baby has to be taught laboriously by its environment in the years following birth.

Apart from a complete system of reflexes for the execution of the actions necessary for the sustenance of life, the longer embryonic period of higher mammals gives them the whole complement of instincts common to the species. This instinct persists in his action patterns even when the animal is placed in an unfamiliar environment where different action patterns predominate. (Consider the hen which has hatched duck eggs and sees her 'chicks' taking to the water!) The human baby in no way becomes a person if apart from reflex actions (sucking, blinking, etc.) he is not also taught his social action patterns (speech, thought). To use Langeveld's expression, man is dependent upon upbringing. The concept of exo-somatic development therefore also embraces walking, talking, thinking, and all the other skills acquired in human culture.

Besides biological heredity there is also a sort of cultural heredity whereby, through the medium of upbringing, culture is transmitted to following generations. This transmission is to a high degree responsible for determining which possibilities of open heredity are developed within the individual. A child will not even learn to walk upright if it has no human example from which to learn—let alone talk or express itself in the countless other ways of human culture. Its instincts are rudimentary, and are limited to certain basic instincts such as those of self-preservation.

If man evolved from groups living in herds, as the nativists assert, then he has even lost the instinct of preservation of the species. In animals that live in herds, if there is a fight between two animals of the same species, it is broken off immediately when one of the two combatants makes a sign of submission. Fighting serves to establish or reinforce the hierarchy, not to kill other members of the species.

In the terminology of Gordon Allport, the empiricists live in the 'Lockean tradition', or, as I would put it, within the choice pattern of John Locke. The best known feature of this 'Lockean tradition' is Locke's pronouncement that at birth, man is a blank sheet of paper, and that everything that is in him enters through the senses. On the basis of this axiom a discipline of science can develop which may justly call itself the science of behaviour. If we then follow Locke's scientific method, which starts from the assumption that the simple idea is more important than the complex whole, and that the complexity is equal to the sum of the simple ideas, then the path is open for a search for ever simpler situations and the reconstruction of complexities from simple ideas.

Opposed to this there are still people who point out that a cathedral as a whole is the sum of all the bricks and stones of which it is built, *plus* its design, which gives each stone its place and meaning. In contrast to the empiricists and their doctrine of elements or ideas, the personalists occupy themselves precisely with those problems which arise from the design of the cathedral. The design itself is referred to by the terms *Ganzheit* and *Gestalt* (wholeness and form). For our purposes I prefer to call it the personality.

The axiomatic choice of a discipline of science may best be seen in its extreme representatives, who have the courage to accept all the consequences of that choice. Thus we see that already half a century ago Watson claimed that, given a group of healthy babies, he would be able to make of each one of them whatever he was asked. And the educational psychologist Skinner states that it is possible to condition anybody for any job, as long as one follows the Skinner method, learnt from conditioning starved rats and pigeons. All the misery of the world, according to Skinner, may be traced back to the fact that people are insufficiently conditioned to find out what is good-pleasant and what is bad-unpleasant.

Skinner's influence on recent developments in pedagogy is still considerable, although it is declining on account of his most recent exaggerations because people are beginning to realize that even the simplest stimulus within the person has a specific significance. If this significance does not change, no conditioning takes place in man. This is of particular importance to modern behavioural therapy, where purely external conditioning has been abandoned as a method. From the Skinner school of thought, however, there is still a movement in favour of the efficient training of people to do certain patterns of actions, in their jobs and for purposes of research, by means of programmed instruction and subsequent multiple choice examinations. In industry, people talk of 'one-best-way training'. Skinner's sorrow is that we still apply his splendid method in the wrong way.

Only by *systematic rewards* for correct actions and *ignoring* incorrect actions can we produce permanent conditioning. What we actually do, however, is to punish an incorrect action (e.g. by giving a low mark or by failing the student) and accept the correct action as a matter of course (i.e. we ignore it), so that conditioning is directed at arousing fear for incorrect actions, which then tend to surface in consciousness with increasing frequency. Again, industry uses Skinner's 'positive reinforcement', which is employed with some success to raise motivation at work. Nowadays this method is taught on management courses.

Skinner is full of remedies that will supposedly bring salvation to the world. He is an advocate of a totally conditioned society, without aggression and with a planned division of roles each of which brings supreme happiness to those who fulfil them. At the same time he does not bypass the question of who is to determine what is good and what is bad. 'The person who determines that is me,' he once declared on enquiry. In his conditioned world he alone will not be conditioned. Someone, after all, has to remain to programme the system!

Skinner has developed his theory from training previously starved rats and pigeons, which, in order to assuage their hunger and obtain food, broke through their innate instincts and performed all sorts of tricks. This experimental set-up, then, is what Skinner alleges to be identical to the learning process in man. The rat, however, has no intention of doing any Skinnerian tricks if he is not hungry. True, a man may also be prepared to do the weirdest things if it will keep him alive, but unlike the rat he can learn *because he is interested* — in trying to solve a problem of mathematics, for example, or the meaning of a Sanskrit text — *even if he is not hungry.*

It is in the absence of a capacity to distinguish levels of motivation that personalism finds most reason for criticizing empiricism. Nevertheless, despite this criticism, the significance of empiricism-behaviourism can scarcely be exaggerated. The impressive volume of material which almost a century of assiduous behavioural research has produced provides a veritable ocean of simple elements and theories, each of which has been made 'hard' by not strictly objective research. It is then possible to make combinations of these and build, for example, socio-technical systems which in turn will solve equally partial problems.

On grounds of their laboratory research into carefully selected and restricted simple phenomena, the behaviourists call what they are doing 'scientific psychology'. Anybody who fails to conform with the aims and methods *chosen* by the discipline (and hence axiomatic), is outside science and may class himself among the practitioners of literature or of subjective assertions. Every pronouncement must be made 'hard' by reproducible laboratory tests or by statistical research in the breadth-dimension (van Leent).

Some partial phenomena can indeed be researched in this way, but as soon as one takes the whole man in his life situation (not in a situation artificially reduced to a few variables) this method can offer little in the way of enlightenment. I shall go into this in greater detail when I turn to personalism.

For empiricism, Goethe's words in *Faust* apply:

Dann hat er die Teile in seiner Hand,
Fehlt, leider! nur das geistige Band.

(Then he has the parts in his hand:
Alas, only the spiritual bond is missing.)

Indeed, it is unscientific even to look for a *geistige Band*.

Empiricism has given rise to considerable enthusiasm in educational circles. Dewey and his imitators gave a new hope to education by pointing to the goal of a better humanity and a better society. The assumption that man is so flexible that he can be trained for many different jobs leads to an attitude towards matters of careers and jobs that is the opposite of that adopted by the nativists, who believe that through heredity man is predestined for one particular walk of life which is the only one that is right for him. Instead of the nativists' key-and-lock theory we might here speak of a lock-and-key theory. There are a number of locks (occupations) for which a number of keys are needed annually. And those keys have to be manufactured. This is what I call 'directed vocational training', in which all superfluous education is eliminated. Every year we need so many hundred technicians, engineers, economists, teachers, and so on. Don't make too many of each, and condition them to the requirements of their jobs. Diametrically opposed to this again is the recommendation made by the implicit or explicit personalist: bring young people up with a broad scale of possibilities, motivate them so that they become aware of what they want out of life, and show them a way to take the first steps along their chosen path. Vocational training is then the stirrup by which they reach the saddle of their first job; after that, many shifts will take place for which they will be grateful to their 'superfluous' education.

Personalism
I shall have to deal with personalism at somewhat greater length than nativism and empiricism, because I have described the development of man's biography from a personalistic point of view. For this reason I should like first of all to give a general account of the origins and problems of personalism, after which I shall turn to a number of detailed points.

Personalism is the oldest known image of man. In all ancient spiritual cultures man is described as being of divine origin and superior to animals and plants. 'The breath of life was breathed into him and he awoke to self-awareness and freedom of choice.'

Man is directed *at his own future*. Man is always on the way somewhere. His actions are limited by the equipment which he has been able to acquire in the past, but within those limitations he chooses a target for himself. If necessary, he can choose to acquire new equipment. In that, he differs from an animal. Man is *finally directed*. The starved rat can be conditioned — but the conditioning soon wears off. The experimenter has to follow his initial conditioning with reinforcement, something which Pavlov learned from his experiments with dogs. It is the typical stimulus-response situation of the animal. Man, however, can during his maturation replace education from outside by self-education and targets of his own. And he can do this independently of whether or not he happens to be hungry. Moreover, every stimulus has a meaning for him in the totality of his psyche.

Modern personalism or humanistic psychology, as it is called in America, by no means denies the basis of heredity, nor the influence and necessity of educating the helpless and more or less instinctual baby. However it also points out that the curious thing about maturation is that the individual recognizes his biological possibilities — he over-sees his upbringing — and starts to determine *what he is going to do with it*. This means that besides heredity and the influence of environment and upbringing there is a 'third force' necessary to understand and explain the complex behaviour of a human being.

Nativism has the 'fertilized egg-cell' image of man.

Empiricism has an image of man which consists of the maturing individual being absorbed into the community through his own efforts in imitating and adapting, through stimulus and response.

Personalism has the image of man in which the adult individual determines his own path and is always on the way to higher levels of maturity and adulthood.

Personalism stands and falls with the 'third force', as American personalists have dubbed it. The battle for the description of this third force has been fought from various points of departure. Strasser, for example, in his *Fenomen-ologie en empirische menskunde* (Phenomenology and Empiric Anthropology) states that the major question facing those studying human nature is that of the essential structures of man. But what is essential? Is it the same for everyone? In other words, is there a human 'being' as an abstraction, as Descartes believed, a 'being' that can be studied objectively from the outside?

Strasser says: 'Something is always assumed when I begin to philosophize: my existence.' '*I philosophize as someone who has grown up in the culture of the West; when I philosophize, it is always together with earlier thinkers.*'

For the acquisition of knowledge an effort has to be made by the human consciousness, a discovery. But, says Strasser, only that is discovered 'which allows itself to be discovered from a certain standpoint and in a certain manner, and that which is thus discovered is not "the" reality but "an" aspect of reality. Observation, which plays such an important role in objective research, is something different from an impression through the senses; an observation is a question and an action. The question then finds something that can be seen or felt. The questioner already knows what he is asking for; if by discovery he arrives at a phenomenon which he finds essential, that is obvious to him. And what is "obvious" cannot be proven. All proofs, deduction, and reasoning, must finally lead to insights, either direct or indirect. But what has already been seen can for that reason not be deduced from anything else.' I have quoted these sentences from Strasser in order to focus the personalists' situation sharply. For some it is 'evident' that man is no more than a mammal and that he is determined by his heredity. To him, influences from outside are secondary and unimportant—the naked ape reveals himself as soon as you scratch the crust of culture. For others it is equally 'evident' that heredity plays a singularly subordinate role and that man, like the rat, is conditioned by his behaviour. And behaviour is the only thing that such people wish to investigate.

For a third group that same behaviour, as soon as it is viewed over a longer period and outside the laboratory set-up, reveals choice-elements which fall outside the pattern of heredity and conditioning.

The choice between these three points of view depends on whether or not one is prepared to recognize spiritual factors in man. Frankl has pointed out that many people appear to be blind to the spirit, which is of course understandable in a materialistic world with materialistic values. For many the spirit is an illusion.

The road from behaviourism to modern personalism has been a difficult one. During the 1930s the human relations movement arose in social psychology, following experiments carried out by *Ruthlisberger* between 1928 and 1932, from which it had emerged that productivity depended not only on measurable physical factors such as temperature, light or purity of air, but also, and much more tellingly, on the measure of human interest which others took in the work. Real interest and human contact, in those days 'immeasurable' factors, had measurable effects!

In this way the first breakthrough of psychic man into thinking about the behaviour of man in the social field came about. The human relations movement which was the consequence of this had to spend several decades fighting labour organizers as well as researchers, who wanted only to measure and assess what *they* considered to be measurable.

The same applies to Lewin's courageous attempts to open up new areas in social psychology, especially in group dynamics. His laudable efforts were the offspring of a deeply felt sympathy with group situations. In his statements and theories he gets no further than offering mechanistic models, so that much of what he says relapses into a form of pure behaviourism. This is true principally of his so-called field theory, which has since become the main base of modern advertising psychology, which is, after all, not very concerned with what is really going on inside the consumer as long as the result of certain drives and inhibitions is such as to make him buy the product. That Lewin was unable to free himself from the spell of behaviourism can almost certainly be explained by the time in which he worked. He died in 1947, when there was still little appreciation of other possibilities in America. Thus Lewin remained a brave forerunner who only after his death was followed by people who were able to carry on the inner thread of his work.

Carl Rogers went an important step further and tried to make a connection between phenomenological observation and 'empathic' diagnosis. To him it was an ethical standard that he should have absolute respect for the other person as a personality in his own right. The other person may be helped to make his own decisions, to solve his own problems, to determine his own future. Help is only emancipating if six preconditions are met in the relationship between the psychologist and his 'client' (a word chosen in order to make clear that the relationship is one in which advice is being given, not a hierarchical situation). The six preconditions are:

1. The two people involved are in *psychological contact* one with the other.
2. The *client* is in a state of vulnerability.
3. The *therapist* is calm and integrated in the situation.
4. The *therapist* experiences unconditional positive feelings towards the client.
5. The *therapist* experiences 'empathic' understanding of the client.
6. *Communication* of this positive feeling and empathic understanding is possible to a certain extent.

Anybody who allows these conditions to work on him or, better still, becomes familiar with them and practises them in real situations will find himself in quite a different situation from that of reseachers of the Lewin school of thought, who are quite capable of enthusiastically breaking up a children's game in order to establish what effect the frustration thus caused has on the game when it is resumed. The justification given by such experimenters is that one has to put up with such situations for the progress of science. But the putting up always seems to have to be done by the guinea-pigs, not the experimenters.

Rogers has built up an entire school of psychotherapists and what he calls 'counsellors', social workers whose task it is to help people in their personal difficulties and to aid them in their development. His method, the conditions for which have been listed in the six points above, is known as the *non-directive method* of psychotherapy and counselling. Unfortunately this non-directivity has been exalted to the level of a dogma by many of Rogers's followers and taken to almost absurd lengths, something which Rogers himself took care to avoid in the 1960s.

Rogers's aim is to further what he calls 'personality change' and what I prefer to call 'personality development'. This is a development *not* determined by the teacher, therapist or trainer and then imposed upon the subject, rammed into him or continually checked by previously determined tests, but chosen by the subject himself and brought to a successful conclusion by him. The help may only consist of assisting him to understand his own feelings and aims, and of helping him to find alternative possibilities in life situations.

Other personalists are Maslow, Gordon Allport and MacGregor. Gordon Allport has had a considerable influence on personalist thinking both in Europe and in America, chiefly through his little book *Becoming*, which has gone through numerous editions in many languages. The title *Becoming* indicates that the personality never *is*, but is always 'becoming'. It is a 'becoming' process which starts at birth and continues during the whole life, reaching to increasingly high levels of maturity and wisdom.

In the preceding chapters on the human life path the

reader has already found a detailed description of these steps of becoming. It emerges that new tasks are continually appearing, new constellations have to be assimilated and made one's own. Where man fails to take these new tasks upon himself, his spiritual development comes to a stand-still and he is delivered over to the laws of biological development, with its growth, equilibrium, and decline. From this it will be evident that a personalistic attitude to life (although important to the individual's upbringing) assumes a position of central importance during the second half of life, when only the spiritual personality can give new impulses for development. In the first half of life, upbringing and, after adolescence, self-determination lay the foundations for this later continuance of growth in creativity during biological decline.

The scientifically oriented empiricists have accused the personalists of bringing philosophical thinking into psy-chology. That is certainly true, and it is even something that personalists consider essential in order to arrive at complete models and statements of problems from working with fragments of psychic life. Moreover, the method used suc-cessfully for the inorganic world need not necessarily be the right method for dealing with the human soul.

Chorus writes: 'Our conviction is that we can know nothing better than man, while we can know nature only on the surface—by describing, observing and establishing connections which we do not understand in their real nat-ure. Scientific knowledge is, as Haering indicates, *a resig-nation-step in human knowledge*: a form of knowledge which we accept because we can go no further.' Well then, reasons Allers, with regard to an object of knowledge such as man it would be wrong to resign oneself to nothing more than scientific knowledge, as the study of man allows a further step in knowledge, namely, that of insight, of *understanding from the inside (Verstehen)*. The primacy of knowledge lies in understanding with insight: 'As far as it is *possible* we must try to understand or see into something psychologically; *only when every means of psychological understanding has been exhausted* can we be satisfied with establishing facts and factual relations at a purely scientific level!'

Turning to the American school, let us now examine Abraham Maslow (1908–70). His most important book is *Motivation and Personality*, first published in 1954; in 1970, the year of his death, a second, completely revised edition was published, with an extensive foreword by the author in which he gives an account of the development of his thinking since 1954.

It is conspicuous that while until then the image of man used by the clinical psychologists had been built up principally through the study of the sick, Maslow's main efforts were directed at studying the healthy personality. I should like here to quote certain passages from his chapter on Personality (pp. 292–93).

The concept of the well-adjusted personality or of good adjustment sets a low ceiling upon the possibility for advancement and for growth. The cow, the slave, the robot may all be well-adjusted.

The super-ego of the child is ordinarily conceived of as introjection of fear, punishment, loss of love, abandonment, etc. The study of children and adults who are safe, loved and respected indicates the possibility of an intrinsic conscience built on love identification, the desire to please and to make others happy, as well as on truth, logic, justice, consistency, right, and duty.

The behavior of the healthy person is less determined by anxiety, fear, insecurity, guilt, shame, and more by truth, logic, justice, reality, fairness, fitness, beauty, rightness, etc.

Where are the researches on unselfishness? Lack of envy? Will power? Strength of character? Optimism? Friendliness? Realism? Self-transcendence? Boldness, courage? Lack of jealousy? Sincerity? Patience? Loyalty? Reliability? Responsibility?

Of course the most pertinent and obvious choice of subject for a positive psychology is the study of psychological health (and other kinds of health, aesthetic health, value health, physical health, and the like). But a positive psychology also calls for more study of the good man, of the secure and of the confident, of the democratic character, of the happy man, of the serene, the calm, the peaceful, the compassionate, the generous, the kind, of the creator, of the saint, of the hero, of the strong man, of the genius, and of other good specimens of humanity.

... How do people get to be unlike each other instead of like each other (acculturated, ironed out by the culture, etc.)?

... The tastes, values, attitudes, and the choices of self-actualizing people are to a great extent on an intrinsic and reality-determined basis, rather than on a relative and extrinsic basis. It is therefore a taste for the right rather than wrong, for the true rather than the false, for the beautiful rather than the ugly. They live within a system of stable values and *not* in a robot world of *no values at all* (only fashions, fads, opinions of others, imitation, suggestion, prestige).

Frustration level and frustration tolerance may very well be *much* higher in self-actualizing people. So also guilt level, conflict level, and shame level.

Child-parent relationships have usually been studied as if they were only a set of problems, *only* a chance to make mistakes. They are primarily a pleasure and a delight, and a great opportunity to enjoy. This is true even for adolescence, too often treated as if akin to a plague.

This is not the place to go into Maslow's theory formation (his holistic-dynamics) in any great depth. The interested reader is advised to read Appendix B in *Motivation and Personality*. It is interesting, however, to note that Maslow calls the inner nature of man partly instinctoid, inasmuch as the inner life is influenced by heredity and has a tendency to remain in existence throughout life. This instinctoid nature of man embraces his primary needs for living, and his temperament as influenced by damage inflicted very early, even during pregnancy and birth.

> In any case, the 'raw material' is more important here than the finished product made by the individual, other people and the environment ... This raw material gradually becomes a self as it comes into contact with the world outside and interacts with it ... A life history is made up of emerging *possibilities*, which are either formed or strangled by external factors.

However, the adult personality is also a creation of the person himself. Maslow says: 'We can no longer think of the person as being completely fixed by forces outside of him.' The person, in so far as he is a *real* person, is his own chief determinant. Each person is in some part 'his own project' and makes himself. Maslow goes so far as to say that 'The normally developing child knows better than anyone else what is good for him, if he is allowed to make his own free choice. So respect what the child chooses for himself and don't dictate too many conditions.'

Man grows further as a person through aesthetic experience—through creativity and especially through aesthetic peak-experiences, and through interest in the world as a whole.

Here Maslow distinguishes between the creativity of a special talent (for mathematics, music, etc.), which is strongly dependent on heredity, and the self-actualizing creativity that comes direct from the personality and is widespread in day-to-day life. Self-actualizing creativity, that is, creativity originating in the individual's own personality, is expressed in every activity, in housekeeping, teaching, and so on. Where the individual also has a special (hereditary) talent at his disposal, it, too, may be expressed in the same actions, but not necessarily. There is a type of person that grasps hold of a more or less pronounced talent and a type that decides to keep the special talent for leisure activities, such as a hobby, and chooses something completely different as work. For Maslow, every role, every activity, and every occupation can be either creative or non-creative.

If we allow the basic thoughts of the American person-alists to pass in review, we are struck by the fact that they are all struggling with a definition of the concept of per-sonality. The true phenomenologist will not even try that, since for him the subtle reality of the person can only be approached from many angles, which must be provision-ally described as penetratingly as possible. The humanistic psychologists go one step further and try to see where recognizably hereditary characteristics may be found, where the environment has had a formative or distorting effect, and where, finally, they may find phenomena which deal with these factors in sovereign fashion, from a new dimension, designing their own future.

2. Psychotherapy and the Image of Man

The image of man upon which psychotherapists and others base their views of the human being and their judgements about healthy and disturbed spiritual life always depends on a choice that is evident to the chooser and is seldom seen as requiring proof as it appears self-evident. Every choice of an image of man has a philosophical character. And with the waning of religious philosophies the choice of a psy-chotherapeutic school of thought has for many people taken on a pseudo-religious character, and has become a sort of faith.

A small incident may illustrate this point. During the mobilization in Holland in 1939–40 some 20 psychiatrists, as medical officers, worked together in the army's psychiatric unit. During one of the daily discussions about the patients who had been hospitalized it fell to me to give an account of a particular patient. I gave my opinions as to the symptoms and, turning to a psychoanalyst friend, ended with the words: 'That is how I see it. If I were to look at it from the point of view of *your* philosophy, I would have to describe it like this: . . .' — and proceeded to do so. To my surprise, my friend the psychoanalyst was more than a little annoyed with this last remark. 'Psychoanalysis isn't a philosophy; *you* are the one with a philosophy, not I.' 'Oh yes?' I replied. 'Then what *is* psychoanalysis if it isn't a philosophy?' 'We have no philosophy — we just tell things as they are!' 'And precisely because you think you tell things as they *are*, that's a philosophy,' was my reply.

For many psychotherapists their choice has a *being* character. After all, isn't it *evident* that man is no more than an intelligent mammal, or a socially conditioned being, or an individuality which chooses itself and creates its own world?

Tied up with the philosophical nature of schools of psychotherapeutic thought is also the intolerance with regard to others. He who attacks my faith attacks my security and must therefore be countered. It is only when one accepts that each school of thought uncovers a particular part of the reality that it becomes possible to study each school with interest and try to locate it in a wider context, which of course is itself no more than a fraction of the reality of 'man'. The study of man is a study with a receding horizon. Every time one makes a little progress one finds that the horizon has also shifted, thus revealing a new field of problems. Every consideration of man is a momentary glimpse of a developing picture. After many millennia of theological images of man, in which the spiritual creation of man preceded his physical incarnation, an approach to the problem of human nature appeared almost within a century, in which physical incarnation is in the forefront, and consciousness and self-awareness have arisen more or less as the happy side-effect of a selection process. By reduction of the totality of the phenomenon of man to chemical and molecular processes or, in psychology, to drives and desires, it became possible for extreme reductionist images of man to be created.

In psychotherapy there are a number of milestones which may be pointed out here, each one of them understandable when we consider the biography of the founder of the school.

Freud

Freud wanted to see the human psyche explained only in terms of mechanisms comparable to the processes of physics and chemistry. In this he was a child of his time, and of the paradigm of Müller, Brücke and Du Bois-Reymond, who in 1842 jointly swore an oath that they would henceforth only allow the chemical and physical process in man to count. As those in charge of the Prussian Academy of Sciences they were in a position to impose their paradigm on their contemporaries and followers. (See Verbrugh, *Geneeskunde op dood spoor*.)

Psychoanalysis has the great merit that it has demonstrated the existence of another consciousness than the ordinary waking kind. Freud's image of man recognizes the id, the pleasure principle, as the essentially unconscious combination of drives with the sexual drive at its centre as the all-powerful *libido sexualis* revealing the essence of man.

The ego, which has consciousness, which observes both inwardly and outwardly, is the principle of reality in man which has to adapt itself to external social reality and therefore finds itself in constant conflict with the pleasure principle, the id. Freud says that the ego is the rider who has to keep the power of the horse, the id, in check.

Third, Freud recognizes the 'super-ego' or ideal ego, which has no reality but is the result of the commandments and prohibitions which have turned the child, as part of the culture in which it lives, into an 'educated' person. The parents play a particularly central role in this indoctrination process. The super-ego, too, is for the most part unconscious and exercises its influence on the ego from the unconscious. Thus the ego stands between the reality of the id, the pressure of the super-ego and the demands of the social life surrounding it.

Man is not permitted to live out his drives to the full! Social and cultural taboos of religion and convention impose standards to which man has to conform. In this struggle for its own existence the ego often has to suppress the impulses of its animal reality, but via detours the animal in man contrives to come into its own and works as a suppressed complex from within subconscious levels. In this it is chiefly the super-ego which acts as a censor and provides the resistance against becoming conscious.

The suppressed drives emerge as *Fehlhandlungen*, faulty or erroneous actions, such as slips of the tongue, slips of the pen, mistakes in general, and so on—and especially in dreams.

Through Freud's technique of *Traumdeutung*, or the interpretation of dreams, the images experienced in dreams are explained in terms of the pleasure principle of the Freudian image of man. The now familiar process of psychoanalysis, the patient lying on a couch with the analyst behind him and outside his field of view, is the concrete elaboration of this technique. Thus an orthodox psychoanalysis, which generally lasts years, with several sessions a week, turns into one great indoctrination into Freud's image of man.

Compared to the strict and dogmatic Freud, his colleague

Adler took a different direction. Those who remember meeting him remember a short, rather fat man with a delightful Viennese accent who would expound on any subject under the sun until far into the night, all the while, almost as if he had a tic, flicking the cigar ash from his waistcoat. Adler's 'individual psychology' sees the individuality of man as the unity and specific nature of human personality, which is indivisible.

The great difference between Freud and Adler is that Freud, like all scientific thinkers, thinks *causally*. He seeks the causes of problems in the past, preferably, in his case, in earliest childhood. Adler, on the other hand, is *finally* oriented. To him, the individuality is turned to a target in the future; problems arise when this target is inaccessible. This target is determined by the balance between aggression on the one hand and the community spirit on the other. Adler is thus finally or intentionally oriented; instead of thinking in terms of cause and effect, as does Freud, he is more inclined to think in terms of means and ends. The most important feature of a person is his individual aim in life, which Adler calls the *Leitlinie*, the guideline. But even Adler sees man as a being of drives, even if the guiding drives are seen to be different ones. Here there are two polarized drives which determine the human life path: the *community instinct* and the *instinct of aggression* or, in other words, the drive directed towards the service of the community and the drive aimed at promoting the interests of the self-seeking ego. When the individual realizes that he is unequal to his ideal, feelings of inferiority develop which may grow to become complexes.

Adler finds hereditary aptitude factors so insignificant that he completely disregards them; nothing is created until after birth, in the interaction between individual and environment. In a cold, heartless upbringing the community spirit is suppressed, so that the child becomes isolated from its social surroundings. A feeling of inferiority in a particular physical or psychic field leads to a search for *compensation* manifesting in aggressive drives in other fields. This can in turn lead to an overcompensation of feelings of inferiority or to a flight into an illusory reality — for example by retreating into sickness when the individual feels incapable of facing up to the difficulties of life.

Adler refers to psychic hermaphroditism, or psychic bisexuality. The male reaction to problems is rebellion, revolution; in children it is stubbornness. The female reaction is submission, obedience, industry, meekness.

Every child, boy or girl, can choose one of the two forms of reaction, depending on its own psychic experience of the male or female in its soul. Adler was a particular proponent of upbringing. A warm, loving upbringing with interest taken in the child's personality and creativity strengthens the drive to community. Therapy consists of talking, making the patient aware of his own aims, his *Leitlinie*, and, especially, *Ermutigung* — the encouragement to find ways of achieving one's own objective and to learn to control one's own aggression or assertiveness with a sense of social responsibility. Adler's primary concern was for younger people, and he paid comparatively little attention to the later phases of life. If it is true that at different phases of life the individual's objective takes on different aspects and also goes through a true metamorphosis, then the finding of the *Leitlinie* is seeking the enduring in the metamorphosing objectives.

The Freud-Adler polarity as causal and final thinkers and therapists illustrates yet again my point of departure. Every choice opens up new sectors of reality and at the same time demands different methods of examination and treatment.

The third member of this group is Carl Gustav Jung, the Swiss psychiatrist and faithful collaborator with Freud, who until 1913 was regarded as the crown prince of psychoanalysis. A conflict gradually arose between Freud and Jung which became final when Freud demanded that Jung should swear on oath that he would recognize the *libido sexualis* as the sole motive of all man's actions. Such a dogmatic attitude was alien to Jung's way of thinking and the two men finally split.

Jung then developed what he called *analytical psychology*, in which an image of man gradually came into being in which there were a number of levels in the unconscious: the personal unconscious, the collective unconscious, and the deepest level of the archetypes, which are the same throughout mankind. Jung never worked systematically, preferring in his long life to examine different aspects of the human soul in turn. In this, he tried to approach his work from a phenomenological angle without preconceived theories. This, of course, was only partially possible, for no form of research is conceivable without some ordering principle in which phenomena become a coherent whole.

One of the areas which Jung examined was that of function types. Two rational functions are at work in man, thinking and feeling, and two irrational functions, sentience and intuition. The rational functions allow us to form opinions and value judgements; the irrational functions provide sentience alone, or are consciously sensorily or unconsciously instinctively present in the intuition.

Jung also distinguished between two types of temperament: the extrovert and the introvert. Together these four types and two temperaments form a sort of compass for determining character. However, it was only in later years that he developed the image of man which may be summarized in the diagram opposite.

We have already examined the anima-animus phenomenon in the chapter on marriage. The ego as it were looks through the anima-animus to the individual's own unconscious, and through the persona to the outside world. The persona may be seen as the layer or crust covering the ego.

The persona is formed by our upbringing and by our adaptation to the phraseology, convention and routine of

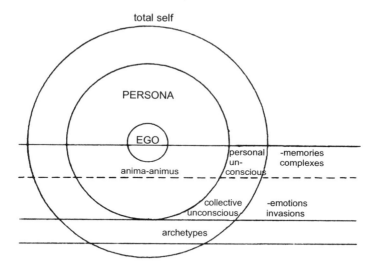

social life. The persona is connected with the typical behaviour expected by the world and is bound up with a particular function.

The solicitor or advocate in a village behaves as a typical lawyer and is seen first and foremost as a lawyer. Few are allowed to look behind this mask (the persona) to see the person behind the function. 'Persona' has a double meaning. First, I look at the world through my persona (there is a great deal of difference between looking at the world as a professor and looking at the world as an unskilled labourer). Secondly, the world sees my persona as my outside, and expects of me behaviour in conformity with my persona.

The persona is at one and the same time a hindrance and protection to the ego, which can hide itself behind the persona in order not to reveal itself.

Another important area that Jung examined was the phenomenon of the shadow or *Doppelgänger* in man's unconscious. Each individual has a shadow, his 'other or darker' side. In this, condensed into a *Gestalt*, is everything that consciousness rejects as being unconscious and inferior in us. The shadow is situated partly in the personal unconscious, the region of memories and repressions, and is connected with the less attractive parts of our life history. To some extent the shadow also has aspects of our collective unconscious and is involved with destructive forces, which are present in every person. Finally, as a *Doppelgänger* the shadow may assume an archetypal character and be experienced as a shadowy brother, split from the person. The experience of the *Doppelgänger* takes place while the person is dreaming; by men it is seen as a man, by women as a woman. It has a repulsive or threatening character, unlike the anima, which appears to the man as a female figure and despite its frightening aspects still points to the positive things that have yet to be achieved. In ordinary life, except in dreams, the *Doppelgänger* is experienced as a projection of the individual's own shadow on other people; the individual's own negative unconscious appears as the behaviour of another, without one's being aware of it. This is where the scapegoat psychology arises — hating other people is really hating one's own projection in others.

To Jung, psychotherapy consisted of travelling a self-desired path of development which he called the *Heilsweg* or the path of healing or individuation. His therapy consisted of dream analyses and especially of making the patient carry out creative artistic work and an extensive study of literature. The limited day-to-day ego, partly conscious and partly unconscious (see the diagram on page 157) had to grow outwards to the self, which consciously contained the total person, the conscious and the unconscious, as well as the region of the archetypes. This path of healing or individuation was seen as a development that continued for the individual's entire life.

In his earlier years Jung expressed his conflict with Freud as follows. Freud has developed his theory on the basis of his patient material, largely young women from richer backgrounds in Vienna during the 1890s; in general they were married to much older men, and their most important problems were indeed of a sexual nature. I myself (says Jung) have had patient material consisting for the most part of older patients, generally over 45 years old; in their case, it was not sexual problems which played a role, but much rather the existential problems of the meaning of life and death.

Like Adler, Jung was much more interested in the final, in the objective of life. If in Adler's concept the objective of life was principally directed at positions in life, Jung, a much more erudite man, believed that it lay in a spiritual development from dependence on the unconscious to an acceptance of the total personality.

Through his study of the archetypes Jung came into contact with ancient Chinese culture and with the cultures of Tibet, India and the American Indians. He travelled widely, and when he writes about primitive cultures he writes from his own observation and does not, as Freud does, speculate on situations with which he is not familiar.

To Jung, an important area for the study of the archetypal symbols and development paths was alchemy. I cannot go more deeply into this here, but anybody who has read Jung's book on alchemy cannot help but feel that his image of man is too deficient to be able to throw any real light on this difficult subject.

It is interesting that ever since his schooldays Jung found it impossible to find any sort of relationship with science and mathematics. This was bound up with his introvert temperament, which could find the way in but not the way out. Jung experienced the world in imaginations, indicating that they are images and symbols for a psychic reality which as such remains hidden behind those images. The essence of the archetypes therefore remains in principle unknowable to Jung, for here there appears a spiritual reality projected into the psychic. Here lie the boundaries of

Jung's work of discovery; the way into psychic phenomena was possible but not adequate to penetrate to their spiritual origin. Jung, for example, went into Goethe's *Faust* but not into his scientific works. Thus he cut himself off from an important path of enquiry and a rich potential method.

In the triad of Freud, Adler and Jung, the last is by far the most comprehensive in his image of man and the most differentiated in his psychotherapy, even though we shall see that he, too, was a child of his time, capable of exploring and dredging an unconscious but not of arriving at an 'upper consciousness' as others did later. Adler and Jung remain prisoners of a psychologism. Jung himself expressly put it that way in a conversation with the psychiatrist Zeylmans van Emmichoven.

With his logotherapy the Viennese psychiatrist Viktor Frankl brought an important new dimension to psychotherapy (*The Doctor and the Soul* and *Homo Patiens*). Frankl, who worked in the wake of Freud and Adler, discusses in his *Homo Patiens* three forms of nihilism in the attitude of man. All three depend on the *reduction* of the total person to an automaton, in a biological, psychological or sociological sense. He calls this *biologism* (what I have called nativism), *psychologism* (my empiricism) and *sociologism*, in which, particularly in politics, man is reduced to being a representative of a class, nation or race.

I have not dealt explicitly with sociologism as one of the images of man. This is, perhaps, the place to say something about it.

Sociologism has gone through a violent revival since 1968 in particular. It is used as a weapon in the polarization of politics and science. One has only to switch on the radio or television, or open a newspaper, to come across such pronouncements as the following. Every psychiatrist, professor, entrepreneur or parent is by definition on the wrong side, being shaped by, and hence a representative of, the existing social order. As such, he must be destroyed. The psychiatrist represents the power of the doctor over his patient, the professor represents power over the student, the entrepreneur power over his employees, parents power over their children. It seems to be the intention of some sociologists that children be educated by correctly indoctrinated and qualified social workers! The most important sociologism of our time is Marxism.

Sociologism, 'man is determined by his social group', is an elaboration, often not even recognized, of Adler's Individual Psychology with its aggressive or assertive drive. True, in Adler's thinking it is balanced by the community drive, but that, in some sociologists' eyes, is only to be found within a given class, and is a drive that operates in an impersonal collective social field. This operation of a collective community drive the Marxist shifts into a future time. When all enemies have been destroyed the earthly paradise will come into being by necessity, because then only people with a community drive will be left; and in peace, without an urge to power, mankind will inherit blessedness.

Political sociologism is always utopianism at the same time. Sociologism in psychotherapy, understandably, expects everything of group therapies.

Now Frankl points out that all three make the mistake of seeing themselves in absolute terms as 'the' dimension which determines the human life-path. The spiritual dimension is overlooked. But the primary spiritual dimensions of life also include the attribution of meaning and the finding of values. To deny the qualities chosen or created by man himself is what he calls 'metaphysical frivolity'. For Frankl the main thing is that each person leads his life 'up to his own truth'. The way to find this meaning to life is to him *Existenzanalyse*, and the therapy 'logotherapy'.

Frankl discusses each of the different meanings of life in a separate chapter: the meaning of life, death, suffering, work and love. He has serious criticisms to make of psycho-analysis with its pleasure principle, and the Adlerians' individual psychology and their power principle. To Frankl, the purpose of logotherapy is to make people face up to their own truth, which is necessarily unique to each individual because no other person can see the world from exactly the same angle. This produces therapeutic reserve in the doctor, and creates considerable responsibility for what happens between *two* people, the doctor and the patient. Only when the person becomes aware of his spiritual dimension in that which he 'ought to become', and finds the path to striving for what he is not yet but what he can be, only then is there any question, according to Frankl, of a genuine, existential therapy. Everything else is merely the biological or psychological treatment of symptoms.

Psychoanalysis is the doctrine of man as something driven (*Es treibt*). To counter this Frankl quotes Goethe's words: 'If we take people as they are, we make them worse. But if we take them as they *should* be, then we turn them into what they *can* be.' It is this 'can be' to which the whole of logotherapy is directed. Frankl writes: 'Human life does not fulfil itself only in work and pleasure, but also in *suffering*. The spiritual is expressed, and longs for expression, in the physical and in the psychic (*seelische*).' And: 'Through love the value-possibility of the loved one is discovered.'

Personal maturation during the course of life is to Frankl discovering and taking upon oneself that which we *can* be. Humour, and particularly the ability to laugh at oneself, plays an important part. At the same time the person is inhibited by the biologisms, psychologisms and socio-logisms, which are just as 'value-blind' as they are spirit-blind. For the spirit in man is a 'personal spirit'. Psycholo-gism, however, looks 'past the spiritual person', while it is precisely the latter which is supreme objectivity according to Frankl. Every spiritual act is intentionally aimed at a meaning and a value. Unfortunately there is no space here to do justice to Frankl's very personal efforts and his logo-therapy.

After Frankl I must mention the Italian psychologist Roberto Assagioli, who, building on the work of Jung and Frankl before him, took an important further step in per-sonalism in his book *Psychosynthesis*. Assagioli was born in Venice in 1888. As a young psychiatrist he was initially a Freudian psychoanalyst, but then went his own way because he felt that psychoanalysis only examined part of the human psyche. From as early as 1910 he worked on a design for what he called 'psychosynthesis' in which both the biological libido of Freud and the human soul itself could be examined. The summary of his life's work in 1965 and 1970 is in the process of gaining considerable influence in psychiatric thinking, particularly in American group therapies. Thus, carried from America on the wings of the humanistic psychologists, he is returning to Europe!

Assagioli has much in common with the humanistic psychologists, particularly Maslow, in that he lays the emphasis on the personality as it is experienced by the person himself, and further on the constant growth and development of the personality and on the responsibility of the self to create its own future through making choices.

Psychosynthesis lays great emphasis on the will of man, not as the driving force but as the regulator and controller of the other psychic functions. The development of the will in this sense is an important facet of his psychotherapy. On psychosynthesis itself Assagioli says: 'It is a scientific con-ception, and as such it is neutral towards the various reli-gious forms and the various philosophical doctrines, excepting only those which are materialistic and therefore deny the existence of spiritual realities. Psychosynthesis does not aim nor attempt to give a metaphysical nor a theological explanation of the great Mystery — it leads to the door, but stops there' (pp. 6–7).

As a psychotherapist Assagioli is here travelling an

unencumbered path. He arouses insights and gets development going, and he goes a long way when he involves Dante and the story of the Holy Grail in his therapy and when he gives meditations with a powerful action. The danger is that it is possible to get bogged down in symbols without a desire to become acquainted with the reality behind them.

It is probably the same here as in other therapies. The many group leaders in psychosynthesis cannot give more than they themselves have. Whoever has failed to find himself a guide to help him open the door, and whoever has failed to orientate himself in the world behind the door will have to stop at the door. His pupils or patients will then, in the end, still have to stay out in the cold — or find another guide.

But despite this, psychosynthesis is an interesting route as far as the door, by far the most worked-out and comprehensive of present psychotherapeutic schools of thought. The most important thing in Assagioli's thinking is that he sets against the lower unconscious a higher unconscious. The diagram of his image of man immediately strikes one as being quite different.

Three areas are distinguished, all of which remain beyond the awareness of the ordinary day-to-day consciousness; only a part of the middle unconscious is contracted to a small horizon of consciousness in which the conscious day-to-day ego stands at the centre. The boundaries of the conscious horizon and the middle conscious area can change depending on whether the individual is thinking of something and brings it within the horizon or forgets it temporarily while busy with something else within the conscious horizon (to this extent the middle unconscious is virtually identical with Jung's personal unconscious, which also contains memories which can again become conscious).

The concept of the *super-conscious world* is important; it is

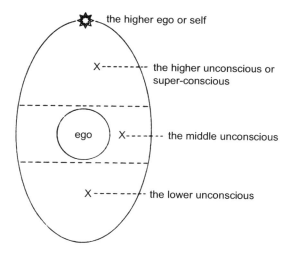

the world in which the intuitions, the inspirations, the 'ethical imperatives' and the urge to noble deeds arise out of the conscious ego. The super-conscious is the source of higher feelings such as altruistic love, of genius, of 'enlightenment' through meditation and contemplation, and of ecstasy. This is where the higher psychic functions and the 'spiritual energy' lie. In the lower unconscious we find everything that rises out of the biological as drives and desires, but also the effects of unassimilated complexes and everything described by the depth psychologists as the collective unconscious and the level of the archetypes. It is everything that is *in* man, but it is not the *only* thing in man! In contrast to depth psychology, psychosynthesis posits an equally real spiritual reality with its own sources of strength. If we place Jung and Assagioli opposite each other as two erudite psychotherapists, we see how in his image of man Jung has no idea of what to do with everything that happens above the limit of consciousness, but simply projects it into the deepest subconscious.

In his tripartite construction of the psychic personality

Assagioli has found a construction which is capable of being used for therapy and which distinguishes qualities and allots them a place. To Assagioli the *higher ego* is a permanently present centre; at each waking from sleep it proves again to be reachable for the ordinary consciousness. In the middle stands the empirical ego which says, 'I want another sandwich,' or, 'I don't think much of that' — and so on.

The *higher ego* is the true centre of the personality, the synthesizing centre, and its permanent presence is the thread which runs through the entire biography. We are unaware of it, but we continuously experience its workings, projected in the soul processes.

The path which Assagioli and his followers and patients wish to tread is the path from the ordinary ego to the higher ego. First we have to get a picture of this higher ego (who am I?). During the course of our lives we must identify our ordinary ego with that higher ego. Frankl put it like this: 'We must turn the truth of ourselves into reality.' And that is a tremendous undertaking! Sometimes it happens through a natural inner growth, but normally we have to work and fight for it for a lifetime.

As an aid along this path, Assagioli recommends that we choose something that can unite the two egos, an ideal which we strive for as, for example, artists, philosophers, seekers after truth; and by our artistic efforts we con-tinuously reach out towards our own truth. It is for this reason that the true seekers in art, science and philosophy are never satisfied — they have never got 'there'. Assagioli is a wise man and indicates many possible paths and gives many warnings and much encouragement. His own path he sees as leading from the multiplicity of the sensory world to the unity of 'supreme synthesis'.

'We seem to feel — whether we interpret it as a Divine Being or a cosmic energy — that the spirit which works on and in all creation creates in it *order*, harmony and beauty, unifying all creatures (some willingly, but the majority so far blindly and rebelliously) with bonds of love, attaining slowly and silently but powerfully and irresistibly the *supreme synthesis*.' In its blessedness this 'supreme synthesis' has an oriental flavour, reminding us as it does of the Nirvana of the Buddhists. Assagioli has assuredly had oriental influences in his thinking.

Assagioli's path is one of inner development, beginning with the techniques of strengthening the thought power, will-power and imagination of the ordinary ego and then continuing into spiritual synthesis, which explores the regions of the super-conscious. When I come to my discussion of Steiner's path of inner development I shall return to Assagioli again. The ground which he treads is dangerous, and not every enthusiastic psychosynthesis group leader is a reliable guide on these paths, especially if unwanted doors suddenly swing open, when it is necessary to be able to distinguish between 'tremendous' illusions and real, controlled spiritual encounters.

The most elaborate and existential form of personalism is found in the thinking of Rudolf Steiner (1861–1925). An Austrian philosopher and scientific thinker, Steiner wrote his *Die Philosophie der Freiheit* (The Philosophy of Freedom) at about the turn of the century. In this book he laid the foundations for his personalistic image of man, later to be elaborated, as it still is today, in anthroposophy.

In the foregoing authors I have described the creators of images of man which have had and are still having a great influence on our entire cultural life. From Freud's biological image of man via the psychological images of Adler and Jung there arose the more spiritual images of man proposed by Frankl and Assagioli. In the thinking of Rudolf Steiner we find an image of man which embodies all three of these aspects at once, so that it does not envisage a separate form of psychotherapy but, instead, a total therapy of body, psyche and spirit.

Steiner's image of man is tripartite. Man, experiencing himself in his psyche, is here a citizen of two worlds: a physical world, in which his body lives, and a spiritual world in which his higher ego lives. In the middle, man experiences himself in the three psychic fields: thinking, feeling, and willing. In this image, the ego lives in a divine-spiritual world, which is seen not as a philosophical abstraction or as the 'sum of human culture', but as the primeval basis of creation. It is here that we must seek the architect behind the appearance of the physical world and the objective of development in man and cosmos.

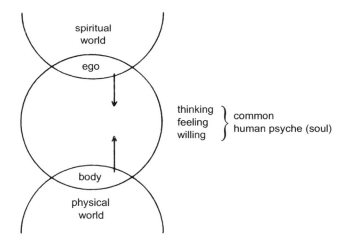

Thus the area of psychologism has been consciously abandoned. Steiner's image of man reaches on the one hand into a divine-created world of corporeality and on the other into a divine-creating world in which the ego goes through its development.

This path of breaking through artificial barriers placed there by scientific division is already indicated in Jung, anchored in religious feeling by Frankl and set as the 'target behind the door' by Assagioli.

It has become increasingly clear to those who listen unrestrainedly to the expressions of the human soul and do not *a priori* impose their own materialistic and biological nature on their observation that the human soul cannot be contained only within the limits of a reductionist psychology. That was the path of development of the psychotherapists named above and of American humanistic psychologists. To Steiner, health in body, soul and spirit is always a balance between two polar forces. For the body it is the balance between growth and decline, which shifts during life so that a healthy toddler has a different equilibrium from a healthy adult or elderly person. To Steiner, therapy is always bodily *and* psychic *and* spiritual; it is always *development therapy*. If someone seeking help goes to a doctor working along Steinerian lines he will first of all carry out a physical examination, at the same time taking note of signs of a shift in a healthy balance between growth and decline. Note will be taken, too, of whether the patient shows signs of premature ageing or of being too young for his age. Here the tripartite biological image of man will be of help. The influence of the consciousness-bearing organs—the nervous system and the senses—furthers decline, while the organs of metabolism stimulate growth. Too much growth in the nervous system results in a lessening of the activities of the consciousness; too much decline in the metabolism leads to tissue dysfunction and hence to decay or degeneration.

In the middle there are the organs that function rhythmically and connect the upper and lower levels. Breathing and blood circulation are both good indicators of balance or imbalance. The therapist will then, through the media of medicines, massage, bathing treatments and so on, together with a regulation of the biological rhythm, be directed towards restoring a balance suited to the patient's age, or, in other words, to *good health*.

At the same time a brief joint record of the patient's

psychic experiences will be drawn up, covering the entire course of his life until the present; it will also cover upbringing, training and the patient's situation in social life. And then begins that which may be termed *biographical therapy*. This consists of acquainting the person seeking help with the usual course of the human biography. Against this background it is then possible to establish jointly what the general problems are which are inherent in the normal crisis of the phase of life and what part of the problem is individual colouring and filling. Generally the separation of normal development problems and the individual problems of the person concerned is enough to provide considerable initial feelings of release. Within the individual problems three things must now happen:

(a) *Physical shifts of balance* must be treated.
(b) *Psychic shifts of balance* must be recognized by the person seeking help, who must be prepared to change his way of life. The predominance of conscious functions of thought and imagination, for example, will lead to sleeplessness, nervousness, even obsessions, while predominance of unconscious impulses will result in the patient's being driven by changing urges, so that new social difficulties will keep appearing.

In the *psychic* field efforts will have to be made to achieve an *active equilibrium*, referred to in an earlier chapter as *equanimity*. To this end a systematic effort will have to be made to achieve open-mindedness and positive thinking (for example, by making the patient write down at least one positive occurrence at the end of the day, and then discussing each event, using the patient's notes, with the therapist).
(c) In the *spiritual field* it is a matter of developing the ego as a spiritual *Gestalt*. The discovery of one's own objective in life, of one's leitmotiv, produces a new 'hole in the future'. For there to be a 'rediscovery' of one's objective in life

something new must be aroused within one's person. Making acquaintance with the human life-path is in itself something new, and is hence sufficient to allow the patient to take a new look at his own life. Depending on the need and possibilities of the person seeking help one is more or less likely to go into the questions of Who am I? Where does my leitmotiv come from? and Why am I going through all this?

The therapist sees this ego as the only permanent thing in man. It existed before birth and will continue to exist after death, enriched by the experiences of this life. This one life is too short and limited to end the path of development. For that, more lives will be necessary, each one with a new leitmotiv as its task. The fruits of the path of exertion and disappointment, of winning and failing, of joy and sorrow, concentrate themselves to a grain of sand. The ego becomes richer, more conscious, and gains more responsibility. This path of development through various lives, this learning process through several 'classes', gives a totally different judgement of the meaning of the human situation in a single life. Heredity and environment are then circumstances that one has oneself desired. Anybody who finds this strange might reflect upon the fact that if, for example, we set before ourselves a target in sport or science, we place well-considered resistances in the training schedule or the study plan that we choose, so that by overcoming each resistance in turn we shall reach higher levels of performance.

The resistances which occur in the biography and which are often considered unjust or give rise to protest are a facet of the biography and hence of the ego itself, and it is precisely because of this that the true leitmotiv becomes apparent.

In the search for the leitmotiv objectives emerge which lie either in the distance or close by. Besides the objective of life itself, *the path to the objective of life* now becomes essential. It is precisely here that the majority of illusions arise. The finding of *realistic aims* on the path to the eventual objective of life is now the central point. Some will tend to seek Utopian aims, so that they will be for ever missing out steps, while others will hardly dare to set themselves a target for fear they fail to achieve it. Finding the happy medium is a virtue learnt as long ago as Aristotle, who said that 'courage is not the opposite of cowardice; true courage stands between cowardice and recklessness!'

From this, perhaps, it is understandable that the balance in the objective can be called the furtherance of spiritual courage, and spiritual courage means the conscious acceptance and further development of the individual's own biography.

With regard to this problem Adler had an *Ahnung*, an idea, though he projected it within unconscious psychological mechanisms.

Adler spoke of the 'arrangement', by which he meant a mysterious power in what was for him the unconscious of the person who arranges 'bad luck' and sometimes even serious 'accidents' for himself, sometimes more than once, just as a good schoolteacher sometimes invents problems or difficulties to help his pupils make progress.

Adler also spoke of *Ermutigung*, encouragement, as an important therapeutic instrument. The difference with Steiner's view is that one ought really to speak of self-encouragement. Thus the biography is at once the path of *individuation* in youth and a continued growth to a *personality* in later life, for the individual *is* an *individual* before he is a person.

Therapy for those seeking help with psychological complaints must necessarily be many-sided. After the physical treatment which has already been mentioned, an artistic therapy with painting and modelling, eurythmy and music will open new worlds of experience, so that eventually the biographic therapy receives the elements for a renewal of the aims in life. The path to these now realistic objectives will have to be trodden with the powers of inner courage, which forms a balance between fear and recklessness. Part of the therapy will also lie in the realization of the new objectives together with others. For we go through our development at all times with and for other people, which is why a connection is sought with other communities. These may be *study communities*, groups of people who come together to help one another in the acquisition of insights and encouragement in the continuation of the development. They may also be *living communities* like families, therapeutic institutes, communes and finally *work communities*. In any case, external performance makes collaboration necessary for others, but in general the individual is not asked for details of his philosophy, nor is he asked to live together with others. The purpose of development can be only one thing: to help each individual to *his own* next stage or level of development. These levels are partly determined by age, which places the individual before ever new problems and challenges. The content of the individual's development is also partly determined by the leitmotiv which the higher ego has chosen for itself in this life and which becomes visible in the totality of his heredity, his upbringing and his reactions to it, or, to put it differently, the way in which he has made use of his heredity and upbringing and how he sets targets for himself for the future. All this can be summarized in the most human of art works — the individual biography.

3. Three Levels of Psychotherapy

If we wish to find our way into the labyrinth of different schools of thought in psychotherapy, it is important to introduce some sort of system into our own thinking. From experience, we may distinguish three levels of approach when dealing with people with mental and spiritual problems. The first of these levels may be termed *mutual help*. This embraces all individual conversational therapies and group therapies, where it is a question of disturbances in the normal life-path brought about by social life and the incapacity of certain persons to find an aim in that life, to maintain contacts with other people or otherwise to maintain their positions. The emphasis here is on 'brotherly' mutual help of the kind which every person can give to every other person.

The second level comprises the field of actual *psychotherapy*. Here we find serious disturbances in the life-path — usually during the critical phases described elsewhere in this book — as well as extreme one-sidednesses in temperament or basic attitude which makes sensible judgement of the situations arising in life impossible. Here too we find the field of more serious disturbances in the life-path, caused by unassimilated remnants from the past and illusory objectives in the future. The emphasis here is on finding new insights and objectives through the medium of art therapy and personal encounter with a therapist. Here the psychiatrically trained doctors should be in control of the curative process.

The third level comprises the field of *psychiatry* proper. Here we are dealing with psychoses. That is to say, the total person in his somatic, psychic and spiritual being is involved in a process of illness. Here the doctor has to determine what therapy is immediately possible and what therapy will be possible at a later stage. Deviations here have somatic foundations. Here the emphasis is on medical therapy (which is not synonymous with the use of psychopharmaceutics!) and other forms of therapy mentioned earlier, but now in a more concentrated form.

If we accept this division into three levels we can put many confusing activities and methods into perspective and see why there is so much variety in this field. It will also become clear where the origins of conflicts lie regarding patients who are treated by one group but belong in another, or who are discharged by one group and not accepted by another.

First, let us turn to the area of *mutual help*.

If a friend in need comes to see me, I begin to talk to him and try to help as best as I can — without any knowledge or experience of methods. Usually this interpersonal help is very effective by itself. The person seeking help has been able to get things off his chest and has found the sympathy of a friend. In other words, he is relieved of his loneliness. Through this type of meeting something new can often be created which overcomes the inner deadlock and allows the person to continue on his path.

This situation of help from another person can be deepened, systematized and professionalized. Professional helpers are now prepared to create situations from which those seeking help may profit. And here begins the labyrinth of helping organizations, societies, groups and individuals. Each one specializes in a certain type of problem, while all sorts of different methods are developed, generally depending on the *helpers'* image of man and society.

Social work, whether or not within the sphere of governmental judicial authorities, exists alongside the free initiative of motivated helpers and social reformers. In addition to the choice of aim or objective the methods and underlying policies play a significant role.

Without even wishing to make an attempt at completeness, I should at this stage like to have a brief look at some of these aims and methods in order to make the reader more aware of the diversity of the field.

There are psychiatrists and psychologists who organize one or two sessions of group therapy a week in addition to their individual therapy sessions; there are institutions for day treatment with group therapy and for family therapy. They all have in common that the participants come of their own free will. If they fail to appear several times running then they are usually removed from the register. In cases of family therapy, if one or more members of the family withdraw, the therapy is abandoned. In this way a sort of natural selection applies with regard to the more severe cases, in which the patient no longer has the initiative or inner possibility of actively desiring his cure.

There are also special reception centres for runaway minors, drug addicts, and alcoholics. Here too, the criterion as a rule is that registration and participation should be voluntary. Then there are many different kinds of 'training': sensitivity training lasting several weeks, *Gestalt* training, psychosynthesis groups, quiet groups (meeting groups), verbal and non-verbal meeting groups or workshops, marathon groups in which the participants stay together for 24 or 48 hours at a stretch, and many other forms of group work with names like xoelapipel, bio-energetics and transactional analysis.

Although enrollment and participation are voluntary, during the sessions themselves there is generally a strong sense of obligation to bring everything out, to express every feeling or sentiment in words and bring it into the group. For more robust characters this pressure can be a help, for those of a more sensitive nature it can be torture. The fact that the individual is quite dependent on a random group of more or less aggressive people requires a great deal of specialized knowledge on the part of the therapist so that each individual can have some protection — some space of freedom. Unfortunately, in spite of good intentions, trainers do not always have this specialized knowledge, largely because in many countries no professional qualifications are required of a group therapist. Anyone who feels like it can set up a group therapy practice.

The quality of group therapy, then, is closely tied up with the quality of the leadership in the group and with the methods being applied. Personally I regard it as essential in group therapy as elsewhere to have absolute respect for the personality *and* the liberty of every participant. Included in this liberty is the right to privacy, the right not to say something at a given moment or in a given group. Heavy pressure and over-long sessions are an assault on this liberty and must therefore be rejected.

Group therapy has gained enormous popularity, and is even, one might say, the 'in' thing. Jubilation at the discovery of the many possibilities of group work has, however, led to an exaggeration of the possibilities and also to a more scornful attitude to individual psychiatric work, which is often concerned with completely different problems which cannot be tackled using the same criteria for treatment and the same methods as group therapies. Psychiatric hospitals are pictured as concentration camps and psychiatrists as obtuse dunces.

But suppose a 'calm schizophrenic' is discharged from a psychiatric hospital with a recommendation that he receive follow-up treatment at a social psychiatry centre. If he still fails to turn up after three reminders, the ex-patient runs a grave risk of being removed from the register, so that some other organization will have to take up his case. By itself there would be nothing wrong in this — a useful division of labour is conceivable — were it not for the fact that the criticism of those other organizations such as hospitals comes precisely from those who failed to provide the follow-up required.

To sum up we can say that group therapies, as a systematized form of mutual help, are a new and still developing field of psychological help. As far as methods go, they are still developing, so that every practitioner swears by his own method. All methods, however, have in common that they lay the emphasis on the 'here and now', on actualizing problems in a group not selected by the patient himself, and that the problems of the biographical development phases play hardly any role at all. The participant 'material' is nearly always in the middle phase of life. The problems of the sentient soul and of the 'vital-psychic strivings' are predominant, purely and simply because of the methods imposed. *Spiritual* problems of a more subtle nature can hardly be looked at, largely because they lie outside the image of man of most group philosophies.

The positive effect of group therapies lies in the removal of loneliness and in the nullification of the results of an insufficiently complete breakthrough from adolescence to adulthood, itself the result, in many cases, of the patient's job and domestic circumstances. In family therapies the problem is to get deadlocked situations moving again and to eradicate preconceived reactions which have crept in. The background of practically all group therapies lies within psychologism, with the possible exception of psychosynthesis groups, which try to provide rather more. But there again it depends entirely on the personality and depth of the group leader.

The second level of psychotherapy, as has been said, embraces a region of more serious disturbances in the biography than those covered by the first level. It is concerned with those people whose biography has come to a halt because of genuine disturbances in their development. Such patients have in common that they no longer have any prospect of a personal *future* with their own objectives; either they are in a state of dull despair or they hold fast to experiences or ways of reacting which they had in the past. A deadlocked biography can only be got moving again if something *new* is added to the existing content of the individual's life, for the primary factor is not the unassimilated past but *the absence of a vision of the future*! As soon as the future again has a point, the past can be objectified and declines in importance in comparison with the possibility of development towards the future.

One of the most important indications for the diagnosis and therapy of developmental disorders is the overall view of the development phases with their inner assimilation of what was absorbed in earlier phases and their critical points. Many people who come to a therapist with developmental problems should be supported in their crisis, as it indicates that the transition to the next phase of life is taking place. Objectifying one's own problems in the totality of the human life-path has a considerable therapeutic effect. It also provides an opportunity for giving specific artistic exercises or selected readings in literature where, for example, the patient's own crisis is described.

Next to the personal encounter with the therapist, artistic therapy is the most important form of therapy at this level. However, it must be individually tailored to the patient. In the collaboration between the therapeutic artist and the doctor a programme must be designed which can then, during the therapy, be modified according in the patient's progress. In regard to anthroposophical medicine, the options are painting, modelling, eurythmy and music. Eurythmy, in particular, has been highly developed for therapy so that exercises can be chosen with great precision for each particular case.

In the psychotherapist's (in this case the doctor's) 'encounter therapy' with the patient, the doctor sees himself as being 50 per cent of the situation. This means that he meets the person seeking help on a basis of equality, as a person, and stakes his own existence in the situation just as much as he expects the patient to do. The therapy to be chosen is oriented finally. That is to say, the analytical phase of the encounter is as short as possible and serves to establish the *status quo*, the therapy's point of departure. Further developments depend to a large extent on the phase of life in which the patient finds himself. In the middle phase of life the patient is more likely to look back on experiences in the earlier stages of life which have to be assimilated during the phase in which the patient is at the time of treatment. This dwelling on the past is kept to a minimum, however, and only serves to make certain specific anxieties or inhibitions more comprehensible. The gaze should soon be fixed on the future again.

Very often the analogy of taking over a shop can be used. If I take over a going concern I also take over the debtors and creditors. There is no point in speculating what might be possible if certain debts did not exist—they do. With the aid of positive possessions a strategy for the future will have to be worked out, and one of the considerations is that certain debts have to be paid. Instead of becoming obsessed by this fact, it is important to stake all one's 'possessions' in order to acquire new ones.

The acquisition of 'new possessions' is the most important aim of therapy for this group. This may mean a general insight into the problems associated with the phases of human life as a whole and of the patients' own phases in particular. It may mean becoming involved in the question of whether one's own image of the world or of man is adequate for designing a strategy for the future, which means discussions and adequate literature. It can also mean beginning to revise one's own task and one's attitude to other people, which may in turn mean participating in carefully prepared and selected group discussions, or taking part in a study group or in painting classes. From the individual encounter with the therapist via intensive preparation the therapy works towards the group encounter, which lies not only on the emotional plane. The liberty and dignity of the person seeking help are prime considerations here, and that means that he must be protected from unwanted breaches of his privacy. For this reason group therapies are often of little use to such patients.

Things are different for those seeking help in the third main phase of life, after the age of 42. Deadlock in this case usually means not having found super-personal values in time. This leads to the patient clinging to his work performance, taking on more and more work and becoming frightened of every younger person who threatens to out-perform him and who is better equipped for the job. The realization that it is steadily becoming more difficult to find a way of adapting in a rapidly changing environment, both at work and in general, is also felt as some kind of threat. This, at least, is the general picture for one group; there is another group which concentrates problems around per-sonal circumstances. The marriage has become empty, the marriage partner is a hindrance on the path to the realiza-tion of illusory objectives in life, the children are getting into evil ways and turning away from their parents. During the forties for women and the fifties for men the menopause causes a staleness of emotional life and alternating feelings of power and powerlessness.

All these problems have already been discussed at some length in previous chapters. We must now consider the path to be taken in solving them.

In every case the doctor will have to carry out a thorough physical examination in order to establish whether there are any hidden bodily disorders and irregularities within organic systems. The patient's daily life will have to be strictly controlled. It will be necessary to introduce a strict daily rhythm and to ban alcohol as a pick-me-up. At this age there is a growing number of people who, though not perhaps alcoholics, are on the road to becoming alcoholics. Figures showing the increase in consumption of alcohol over the past few decades speak for themselves.

The only true therapy for this sort of situation, strange though it may sound, is to find a new spiritual content to life. Where that does not exist, alcohol is the only consola-tion for declining performance and vitality. Psychotherapy for this group therefore consists of stimulating spiritual or artistic activity. Here the doctor can give no more than he is himself, but he has to give himself absolutely. After the patient's daily habits have been regularized, the therapeutic talks take on more of the aspect of friendly chats. The helper becomes the guide in a process of spiritual development. Simple exercises in concentration, practice in observing nature, and the beginning of contemplation of the values of life become the precursors of a meditative life. Going through the literature together, bringing the patient into contact with others who are seeking a path, can give the support he needs to assume a new style of living.

The effect of a new style of living usually becomes apparent in biological ways. Sleep becomes more regular, chronic fatigue declines and turns into pleasant tiredness after useful work. The patient's interest in his job returns, some work is passed on to others, other work more commensurate with the patient's new attitude to life is taken on. If things go well, his relationship towards his therapist will become more informal, so that it is more a question of friendly help and advice from a distance. If things are a little more difficult, the doctor may have to call in his arsenal of artistic therapies, individual therapies and group therapies. Generally speaking, older patients are not suitable material for the usual forms of group therapy, which deal with emotional problems of earlier phases of life.

The reader may be surprised to see so little said about dream analysis for this second category of patients, especially as it played so important a role in the work of Freud and Jung. This has to do with the therapeutic method advocated here. However, in individual cases a dream may be important to an understanding of the patient's own position. In general less attention is paid to the dream content, more to the dynamics of the events in the dream. Apart from that, strength for the future, especially in this phase of life, is drawn from the super-conscious, not the subconscious.

One special area comprises the psychotherapy of retired people who suddenly realize that although they had so many plans for things to do after stopping work they are now failing to achieve anything. Here too, the regulation of the daily rhythm and the general tempo of life is extremely important, alongside stimulating the patient to new creative activity, whether or not connected in any way with his previous life. It may well be possible to embark on some sort of group activity, not so much in the form of group therapy but as tasks to be jointly carried out to meet real needs outside the group. I have already said something about the new pensioners' culture; it is both therapy and an outgoing movement into the cultural life of the local environment.

The third level of psychotherapy comprises true classical psychiatry. Despite the existence of schools of thought which seek the causes of psychiatric phenomena in the psychological only (so-called antipsychiatry) or seek to explain them purely in terms of biochemistry, my own view embraces a *physical* background to such disorders, which therefore requires *medical* treatment and, unfortunately, all too often hospitalization in a psychiatric clinic. There is space here to deal only with a few of the many aspects of psychiatry. Endogenous depressions, the many forms of what has been lumped together under the general term 'schizophrenia', and serious hallucinations or severe feelings of anxiety often cannot be treated on an ambulant basis, partly in the interests of the patient's own safety, partly for considerations of the public well-being, where the task of treating such patients as they deserve *and* carrying on a normal life becomes too severe.

The great problem of patients with serious disorders is their large number, which makes it necessary to have a vast number of doctors, nurses and the like in order to meet the requirements of changing ideas relating to different sorts of therapy for such cases of distress.

Much has already changed. In some cases it is possible to arrange small units in which there is one therapist for every two or three patients and in which it is possible to meet the demands of therapeutic help and resocialization. It will be clear that at present it remains beyond the scope of practical politics to make such arrangements for all patients. The attempts by some antipsychiatrists to organize treatment in open houses in which therapists and socially maladjusted patients work together certainly deserve our fullest attention, but because of their experimental nature and the uncertainty of continuity they cannot yet be considered a solution for the large majority of patients.

In any event we cannot expect all closed wards suddenly to become redundant overnight (see Kees Trimbos, *Antipsychiatrie*, Deventer 1975).

Where therapy appears to be having little effect one is faced by the problem of long-term hospitalization, work therapy, and so on. Where resocialization is possible, albeit at a lower level than previously, one then has the problem of rehabilitation in society. Here again, the official organizations are all overloaded and the patient runs the risk of falling between two stools. True psychiatry is thus a matter of both medicine and considerable social organization.

One of the central elements in approaching the psychiatric patient is that under the delusion, anxiety or rigidity the complete ego-person is always present. If one addresses oneself direct to this spiritual core (bypassing the anxiety or delusion) the ego remains approachable. From my own experience I know that even apparently totally useless one-way conversations can be remembered by the patient for years afterwards. They may therefore have their therapeutic effect long after taking place.

The journey which the so-called schizophrenic patient makes through his inner organic depths can only be compared with the experiences of the medieval mystics, except that they had a long period of religious and mystic training behind them and were therefore in control of their experiences whereas schizophrenics are overwhelmed and imprisoned by them. A therapist with some knowledge of mystic training will be able to help the patient with understanding and with a constructive critical faculty. When the patient has recovered it will emerge that his chief need was for such understanding, non-labelling help, in which the full integrity of his ego remained intact.

The situation here is the same as that of remedial education, where even the most backward of children has a right to an artistic therapeutic environment in which an appeal is made to his highest ego. The comparison of the ego with the violinist and his instrument is valid here. Even a musical genius will be unable to produce very much from a violin with only one frayed string. Yet the defects of the instrument tell us nothing about its player's artistry, which remains capable of expression on an intact instrument.

In 'grand psychiatry', too, we can see the despair of countless gifted individuals who are unable to use their own damaged instruments to communicate with their fellow-beings. It is absolutely vital that in this situation the therapist should take the individuality of the patient perfectly seriously and act accordingly. In practice, this can be difficult. The person who carries within himself an ego which is an independent entity, pre- and post-existent, will find the strength of his convictions to meet these demands to the fullest possible extent.

Luckily there are also patients in psychiatry and related fields who are only disturbed at intervals or who allow a more direct approach during the recovery stage. For them, everything that has been said about the previous two categories of patient also applies, so that they may be involved in artistic therapy, meaningful discussion, friendly encounters and mutual help.

Chapter Seven

Personal Development and Biography

*The human biography is a symphony which each individual
personally composes*

As I have already said on more than one occasion, the
human being can take his biography in hand through his
own actions. Unconsciously or consciously, he can be the
architect of his own fate. In this, a number of points are
important. First, anybody who seeks conscious personal
development will still have to obey the laws of the phases of
development. It is no good wanting to 'flower' before one
has formed enough 'leaves', and leaf-formation is not a
particularly spectacular activity! Secondly, those who seek
inner development have a superabundance of possibilities,
paths and paradises available to them. They will have to
make a choice, preferably on the basis of insight. He who
merely seeks uncontrolled 'experiences', 'expansion of
consciousness' or 'visions' will most simply achieve his aim
by chemical means. Many do just that, at the same time
turning their intoxication into a holy cause, a sort of faith
which they have to carry to the world at large. There are
then the curious, who try it once and then seek other paths,
and there are those who seek refuge from their own
biography in the world of the chemically altered consciousness. This applies equally to alcohol and heroin and
everything in between.

The uncontrolled, chaotic experiences of 'trips' and being
'high' have nothing to do with personal development,
which requires the conscious exercise of faculties that lie
dormant in the majority of lives. I have already pointed out
that man is born with very many possibilities, and that

because of our modern culture only a very small proportion of these are required and hence exploited. It is for this reason that many people feel dissatisfied with the reduced world in which we live as reduced people. But *what* has to be developed? Here the paths separate quite soon.

Part of what is on offer comes from the Orient. From the ancient (and modern) Yoga and Zen Buddhism through Mazdaism to Sufi, to name but a few, there is a wide spectrum of choice. They all have in common that they connect with the roots of our civilization. Here the thinking is: back to unspoiled origins! Become familiar with that which has proved its worth over many thousands of years! Indeed, the richness of these ancient stages of development demands respect. They all have their roots in cultures that may be termed *spiritualistic*. Spiritualism is the philosophy that says, simply: the spirit is all — matter is illusion. Everything originates from a divine process of creation. But matter is allied to the antispirit, to darkness. Free yourself from the temptation of darkness, give up your egoistic ego-consciousness and be absorbed into the divine world of light from which man was born. In other words: go back to the pre-birth, back to paradise, back to the *Vor-Ich-hafte*.

All religions of revelation — and that includes the Old Testament — are founded on divine revelations. In earliest times each and every individual could experience a world of light in a dream consciousness; the last of those who saw that world wrote their experiences down for those who no longer saw it themselves.

This view of inner development is of course contrary to modern historical materialist approaches, according to which sly priests maintained their power over the masses by feigned revelations and sanctions. For us children of the twentieth century it is difficult if not impossible to transport ourselves into the type of consciousness that existed in an earlier spiritualistic era. A final glow of such a time may still be experienced, for example, in Bali, where in gladness and trust a divine world still takes part in everyday activities.

If we look back on the grandiose contents of the ancient religions from the standpoint of modern personalism we see the history of the origin of the human ego, born out of a divine world. But that ego has now become full-grown, and is now a responsible participant in further development. It can therefore no longer stand still in its own 'youth', however glittering and warm it was.

From the roots of our own western civilization in ancient India, Persia, Chaldaea and Egypt, to name only the most important of its sources, Greek philosophy first developed an attitude to life that was new in principle, and may be termed *idealism*. In the work of Plato a world of the gods is no longer attainable for men; man is born of the primitive world of ideas. Knowledge was therefore the remembrance of things known before birth; observation and understanding were recognition. The gaze was still directed to the pre-birth world, to the 'spiritual fatherland' of the awakening ego.

Throughout the Middle Ages until and including Scholasticism, philosophical thinking was primary. 'I think, therefore I am,' Descartes was still able to say at the beginning of the modern age. But the new era which set in with the Renaissance (and not with a 'naissance', with something new) continued to draw on the riches of the Greek world of ideas. Soon the idea shrinks into reason and rationalism is born, followed by mathematism, which seeks to attribute reality only to the ideas of mathematics.

The way was now open to *materialism*, the philosophy which stands diametrically opposed to spiritualism and claims that everything is matter and the effects of material forces. Instead of a divine process of creation the god of 'coincidence' appears, to create ever more complex bonds from simple connections, while growing complexity is supposed to call up consciousness. The spirit is now maya or the Great Illusion.

Let us not deceive ourselves; we are all heavily infected with materialism, even where we seek the spirit in religion or in philosophy. The moment at which the conflict over the meaning of the Last Supper began, when the proof of divinity had to be produced, was the moment at which materialism broke through.

Every philosophy is aimed at something in particular. Spiritualism provides a grand doctrine of wisdom, ideal-ism, a doctrine of ideas, a philosophy of life; materialism is the doctrine of material things. Science and technology have changed the material world, have brought material pros-perity, but have left spiritual needs unanswered. This is something that has become increasingly obvious during the past few decades.

All traditional and institutional churches, which acquired their forms from ancient spiritualism, have lost their meaning for an increasingly large number of younger people, who, *if* they seek something spiritual, seek new paths which mean the development towards a new stage, not a renaissance of the stages of the past.

This search may best be characterized as the need for a new philosophy in which there is a place for both material things and the things of the spirit, in which it is not neces-sary to abandon exact thinking but where the spirit can be incorporated into our image of the world together with everything that our present culture has so laboriously made its own. One might term this a longing for a new form of *realism*. Realism seeks to examine spirit and matter in equal measure and bring them together in a single image of the world, an image born of historical necessity, being the next step on the path of development of western culture. I shall discuss this search for a new realism in my further con-sideration of personal development.

To further examine what is offered as paths of development we must turn our gaze *westwards*. A varied spectrum of personal development paths comes from America, although the paths which it includes are presented as therapies or paratherapies: sensitivity groups, basic encounter groups, marathon groups, *Gestalt* groups. They are all aimed at the development of social faculties in man which have been allowed to lie fallow by our modern culture. This faith in the group, in a sociability as a reality superior to that of the individuality, and the development of the individual into a socially functioning power source, are clear indications of a reaction to the one-sidedness of our culture and as such, when applied with sincerity, can be individually curative. Dubious in these movements is the pseudo-religious character of the therapies, not originally intended by the founders, perhaps, but disseminated by converted adepts who have turned the 'here and now' into a religion.

Yet here too we see a step in the direction of seeking a form of realism, even if the spirit here is still very abstract and shadowy, being present only in a human 'personality', so that the spirit itself remains somewhat vague as to its origins and future. Even in the work of Frankl and Assagioli, who posit a super-ego functioning in an area of the spirit, the image of man remains close to being a psychologism, so that we are obliged to wonder whether the spirit is reality or really the acquired content of our culture.

The Orient offers us many paths—back to the pre-birth, to before the Fall. It offers a grandiose wisdom to be found in ancient books and traditions. But alongside the great religions and their contents the ancient development had a second, more hidden stream which had its chief effect in cultural life. This was the stream of the ancient 'Mysteries'. The Mysteries were anciently the training-grounds of seekers after wisdom, and particularly for those who had to provide leadership for their culture. By means of lengthy physical, mental and spiritual exercises the Mystery-pupil was prepared for his initiation, in which he went through an experience akin to death, to the experience which the dying man has when he loses his body.

Brought back to life before the stage of actual death was reached, the initiate was now a 'twice-born'. Death no longer held any horrors for him, the certainty of a spiritual existence had now become reality to him.

But the Mysteries were more than that; they were very much aimed at the future development of mankind. Faculties such as abstract thinking were practised there, long before they had become the common property of the culture; mathematics, astronomy and medicine were all practised in what was for that time a future form. We know that for 30 years Pythagoras visited a number of Mysteries before he made his mathematics known to non-initiates, and Hippocrates in his time was the leader of a Mystery school on the island of Cos. Social forms, too, were reformed from within the Mysteries, often colliding with the traditional forms of an old spiritualist religion of revelation.

At the height of the Greek era the Mysteries were still flourishing, the centres being Samothrace and Eleusis. All the great philosophers were initiates. In a certain sense the Mysteries can be called the 'spiritual universities' of antiquity. Although the content was kept strictly secret, the results became apparent in the culture.

Does Europe, lying as it does between east and west, have anything new to offer for the future realistic image of man and the world? The path from materialism to realism (to re-establishing the reality of the spirit) is not a single leap of mutation; there are a number of intermediary stages. Goethe's phenomenological consideration of nature in his plant metamorphosis and especially in his theory of colours, Wundt's sensualistic psychology with his activity in observation, and Leibniz's monadism are all intermediate steps on the way to overcoming the 'materialism of coarse matter'.

Phenomenology, above all, is a useful method for discovering phenomena that require a different explanation. Thus the phenomenological study of natural phenomena, the 'penetrating description' of them without preconceived materialistic ideas of them, is a way of orienting oneself in the phenomena of life. Phenomenological psychology and studies such as those by Buytendijk on men and animals and Portmann on the animal are also ways of gaining access, in a modern manner, to human essentials.

But not everybody will be able or willing to travel this path; and for those who are not, there is a possibility of getting to know their own interior through practice. The conditions for this are: the creation of moments of inner peace, concentration exercises, striving for equanimity in emotional life, practising positive thinking when acting. Concentration and meditation bring order into the world of the imagination and carry on the thinking of the great leaders of our western culture. For some, the path will lie in the *Imitation of Christ* by Thomas à Kempis, for others in Dante, *Parzival*, or Goethe's *Faust*. Occupying oneself with the contemplation of the Gospels brings a new inner world to life. Also occupying oneself with the laws of development in plant, animal, man and biography leads to greater insight and more social skills than concentration on the feelings of 'here and now'.

A different path has been taken by the analytical psychologies and therapies. Here, in a path of discovery lasting many years, in 'analysis', man's own subconscious has been raised into consciousness. During this process it has become apparent that in indicating what has become conscious the analyst's own image of the world plays a decisive role. For some this will be a biological primal drive, for others it will be seeking a place in the social environment, or a remembrance of the deepest and most ancient symbols. For yet others, a cosmic world is reflected in the depths of the soul. What strikes one is that they all (as discussed in the previous chapter) look inwards to the individual's own inner feelings and the improved functioning of the conscious person.

The paths of development nowadays available to modern man from oriental schools of thought, analytical treatments, group therapies and the like are all founded on the way inwards, on increasingly deep introspection.

In antiquity the Mystery-pupils were taught that on this path inwards man encountered the gods in man, but also the deceivers and the demons. It was the task of the hierophant of the Mysteries to see to it that the pupil did not descend into the unconscious regions of his own psyche until he had an idea of what he might meet there and until he had learnt to distinguish between wishes and desires rising up in beautiful and repulsive images — and between hierarchical beings called angels, archangels and so on in the Bible and other names in other cultures. They are experienced inwardly as images of a superior reality, in forms borrowed from a sensory world, with attributes relating to their tasks and beings. One only has to go to the Egyptian or Assyrian department of a large museum and see the 'imaginations' of these hierarchies hewn in stone, or to look at medieval paintings, to realize that to these artists there was another world every bit as real as our sensory one.

The inward path and its consequences for modern man is described by Jung when he relates how in 1913 he reached the stage at which he decided to allow himself to 'fall' into the depths of his subconscious, without knowing whether he would come out of it as a normal person or as a lunatic. He felt that he was obliged to take this risk in order to better understand his patients, especially the so-called schizophrenics among them. Jung spent many years working systematically through his 'descent into hell', painting and describing the images so that he would be able to use them consciously. Whoever fails to do the latter will fall prey to the negative forces of the unconscious, says Jung. In those years he wished he had a 'concrete guru, one standing above the problems, knowing and capable', who would have disentangled the involuntary creations of his imagination.

The risk which Jung took would never have been permitted the pupils of the ancient Mysteries. A pupil was only allowed to travel that path when he had been sufficiently prepared so that he could distinguish between sham and reality, temptation and task. For modern man the unprepared path inwards is full of dangers for the spiritual equilibrium. Many, therefore, like Jung before them, seek a guru, a leader, to help them on the path.

But for modern man a new path has been opened. One positive consequence of the scientific and technological age is that we have learnt to observe and investigate. True, science as it has developed so far has put on spectacles which only allow certain observations to be made with its equipment and which because of its materialistic theories only accept limited explanations, but this can change. The method of intensifying sensory perception and testing its consistency can also be used for non-materialistic sciences.

Phenomenology is the first step along this path. The first great phenomenologist in the field of the plant world was Goethe. Through endless and increasingly intensive observation there arose before his mind's eye, through condensation, a picture of the primaeval plant, from which according to the working of *Metamorphose und Steigerung* (metamorphosis and intensification) all plants are capable of developing. According to many people this primeval plant is nothing but an idea, but to Goethe it was 'an idea which I can see with eyes'. I would call it an 'objective imagination'.

This *path outwards*, where the form-creating world is perceived *in* the observed object, is a path of development which was elaborated further by Rudolf Steiner in what he called 'Goetheanism'. The research methods involved require a different equipment and orientation as for example sensitive crystallizations, and give clues as to other qualities of drinking water, food, plants and medicines than the usual chemical means do. At the same time this path leads to a refinement of diagnostics, therapy and teaching in education and remedial education. It is a path, still to be described fully, of striving towards imagination, inspiration and intuition. It does not examine primarily the individual's inner world and his own complexes and inhibitions but the world outside, so that it can be seen as spiritually permeated. From that starting-point it is then possible to develop a new form of social action in medicine, agriculture, education, remedial education and psychotherapy.

After this the *inward* path assumes quite a different meaning. The individual's inner world has now become a field capable of being researched objectively, with the methods now acquired. This is less exciting than the paths offered by the ancient doctrines of wisdom, which have now in many cases become vaguely mystical, and it is also less emotional than the experiences that are brought to the surface by group therapies. But one knows what one is doing and can progress step by step in the clear light of controlling thought.

I have often been asked why it is necessary that man should concern himself with such profound, weird and evidently dangerous things as the exploration of unconscious regions and the search for a reality behind reality. Why can man not be content with the measurable and observable sensory world? There is surely enough in that to be researched by ambitious young scientists. Why does everything have to be made so difficult? We have just got rid of a lot of superstition. Let us not now introduce a new superstition of 'superior forces'.

The answer to these questions is very simple. Anyone who is satisfied with the reduced image of man as the naked ape is welcome to it. We shall see that with such an image of man the individual is capable of successfully passing through the middle phase of life, but that in the final, third phase of life he is likely to find himself in difficulties. The biological-materialistic image of man offers no more than a future picture of biological decay, a falling-off of everything that once gave pleasure or even had some value. This is the weak side of Bergler's book, which I have praised elsewhere, about the 'illusion of second youth'. Man in his fifties must have no more illusions, but must reconcile himself to the fact of a life being extinguished. In essence he is faced by a void, and must accept the fact. For those who prefer to take up that stance in life, a whole phase of life, for many people the most important one of them all, remains a closed book. From that same 'book' many others draw the possibility of wresting themselves free of the biological decline and adding a new, creative dimension to their biography.

This is where there is a parting of ways. It is difficult to have a discussion between people experiencing different realities.

An inner development path
'In every human being there slumber faculties by means of which he can acquire for himself a knowledge of higher worlds'. This is the first sentence of Rudolf Steiner's little book *Knowledge of the Higher Worlds*. After 50 years of studying Steiner's works I can now state that here lies a path to a new realism. Whoever wishes to follow this path will have to relinquish the desire for quick results like 'widened consciousness' and 'shining experiences'.

As described, starting from modern scientific methods and working systematically we move along a path on which abstract thinking becomes 'imagination'; here, reality is revealed to the thinker in images that hold a greater content than the definitions.

Emotional life acquires an inspirational character when

one practises an art not for the result but for the training which it gives in perceiving the reality behind external appearances. Music and the world of colour are most likely to open the door to such training.

The life of the will gains an intuitive character; 'presence of mind', in the literal sense, is here the fruit of exercises of the will. It is distinguishing between the essential and the non-essential, the intuitive act.

The consequence of an imagination is an insight into a more profound truth; the result of inspiration is an approach to beauty; of intuition, the creation of goodness, the right (good) action for the situation. Such a path can guide man through his biography. In adolescence the young person becomes aware of the puzzle of himself and of the world; the tendency to plunge wholeheartedly into ideals is great, patience is still undeveloped, the under-estimation of opposition disturbing.

Nevertheless, the seed can already be sown which will grow during the biography into a more complete plant, the flowering of which may not take place until 40 years later.

During the twenties the energy for tackling one's own development is present in full; experience with the internal and external resistances leads to a healthy sobering during the thirties. The danger is that this sobering or disillusion will lead to the individual giving up the path as such; life is so full, and provides the urge to learn first and foremost from experience.

But round about the fortieth birthday the decision whether or not to continue with inner development becomes existential and decisive for the course of the third main phase of life, as we have already seen. Even where no systematic meditative path is chosen it is a matter of fulfilling oneself with contents other than materialistic ones. Literature, art and social responsibility can all bring true inwardness even at this relatively early stage.

In the second half of the fifties the construction of a

second inner world alongside the world of work becomes an urgent necessity. So often I have had to ask people in responsible positions what they would do if suddenly, for whatever reason — an accident, for instance — they were to lose their jobs. So often the answer was that there would be nothing left for them. At the moment when a person says that, he sees before him a void which he is still carefully walking around.

It is never too late to embark upon a path of inner development. If one begins at 18 one has many illusions but a longer period in which to arrive at realism; if one begins at 60 one has vast resources of experience and will be able to orientate oneself more quickly because one already knows much unconsciously.

The path of inner development has its own consequences with respect to the community and the culture in which the individual finds himself, and with regard to the individual himself and the higher world. The personal development of the individual leads to what Neumann has called life from within, the 'inner voice'; one becomes a 'heretic of the inner voice'. Our life is no longer guided by what words, conventions and routines make us do and think, but by the inner voice, by a *beginning intuition*.

The 'heretics of the inner voice' are the hope of our culture. They are always persecuted and always will be persecuted. In the past they have been given poison cups or been burnt at the stake; nowadays they are ignored. Socially, they are the troublemakers, the ones who are dissatisfied with what exists. Since there are many inner voices, and since even from the standpoint of nihilist philosophies of violence Utopian paradises on earth are promised, the path of the middle, of contemplation and inner discipline, becomes all the more necessary for the future.

The golden rule of inner training is chiefly a social one: avoid 'polarization'; know that reality is both good and bad, and that every problem lies somewhere between two extremes.

With regard to oneself the path of inner training begins with the creation of a rich inner life, of being open to philosophy, religion, science, art, nature, education, and so on. It is only in this rich inner life — which can also reveal itself in the quiet of nature, for it is not the quantity but the profundity of experience that is important — that a life of concentration and meditation can be carried on to any useful purpose.

Personal development irrevocably places the individual before the question of whether there really is a higher world, or whether it is an abstraction or projection. Here it is impossible to give advice, for each individual must arrive at his own certainty, whichever way it turns out. While on the inner path, many people come to the certainty of an objective spiritual world in which the human ego has its home.

Finally, one of the questions which we ask ourselves as adolescents, 'Who am I?', occupies an increasingly central position in our inner development. Not because we wish to revel in our own importance, but because we want to know 'what we really ought to do'. Here too, various answers have been found. Schiller once wrote in a letter to Goethe (who lived almost opposite him, but in those days people still wrote letters!) the following, freely translated:

If I get tired in the evening in the middle of writing a letter and put down my pen and go to bed, the next morning I find the half-written letter lying on the table. In that, I am not free. But I am free to tear up the letter and throw it away, or to finish it and send it. That is where my freedom lies. Might it not be just the same with human life? Do we not find many unfinished letters on our path through life?

If we think this image through, we find a possible answer to the questions of 'Who am I? Where do I come from? What is my real task? Where am I tied down, where am I free? Where do I stand in relation to the unfinished letters which I, too, find on my path through life? Do I have to do everything *myself*, or am I part of a network of connections and relationships that will *also* give me love?'

The answering of all these questions finally determines the individual's *élan* and his faith in the composition of his own biography.

In our society we stand on the threshold of a new era. Materialism is certainly not the last of the world philosophies. The true task of our time must yet be completed, and it is just beginning to become visible.

At one time when a man looked outwards he saw a divine-spiritual world, and when he looked inside himself he found the same thing. But because of that, interest in a material world was slight. Gradually the view of a divine-spiritual world was lost. The gods were no longer visible — the twilight of the gods had begun. They could only be experienced in initiation into the ancient Mysteries. The prophets who last looked upon them were replaced by the scholars of scripture, who spent their time discussing the prophecies. The philosophers brought independence to human thinking, but could not themselves look upon the gods. Between the divine world and the sense world a threshold had been thrown up which for a time could be bridged by faith.

But with regard to the individual's own inner world, too, alienation set in; here too, a threshold was created. What the last of the mystics were able to experience of a divine world in their own unconscious became a world of blind organic drives which were only recognizable in a chaotic dream world to later 'scientific' investigators.

Both outwardly and inwardly the honest person of today stands before a threshold over which he cannot pass. Faith and dream images have faded. In utmost loneliness he can find only in his own ego the strength to find a path by which he may pass across the two thresholds. What used to be given to him he now has to develop for himself. He can no longer wait passively, but has to actively search. His image of the world in a sense world has become a surface consciousness; he sees shapes and movements, he can develop hypotheses and theories that make it possible for him to manipulate the created world and its laws and make new combinations from old, but he cannot make a single pronouncement about the *being* of things. 'Ontological questions' may not even be asked any more — they are unscientific. He has become a master at killing, but stands before a wall which, like life, must not only be described in its external features but must also be seen through into its reality. He can create no life, explain no consciousness, test no values.

The path over the threshold to the outside will only become possible if he develops new faculties, faculties which lie dormant within him but which have to be aroused and practised like every other faculty. This means that perception calls up not only a photographic image but also a meaningful image, an imagination.

In this, the artist shows us the way. A true work of art is already born of experiences on the other side of the threshold. It is at one and the same time present to the senses *and* a revelation of a meaning. One step further, and the creative forces themselves become recognizable, revealing a spiritual background of natural forces. Science, art and religion, separated into mutually exclusive fields by our materialism, will have to be reunited. First of all, science and art must become friends again in their methodology, and the 'scientist' vision must give the artist insight. Only then will a new 'religion' be awakened; that is, literally, a reunification with a divine-spiritual world.

Goethe said:

Wer Wissenschaft und Kunst besitzt
Der hat auch Religion.

With these words he indicated the aims of his phenomenological method. The sciences can and must become new Mystery sciences, spiritual sciences. Then technology will again be able to serve life. We shall not only have to combat the destruction of the environment; we shall have to become environment-creators.

On the other hand the path inwards will have to lead in a new way over the threshold to a divine-spiritual world *within* us. Biological drives become divine gifts, originating in a long spiritual evolution. They must not only be 'accepted and lived out', but also developed further to new and superior forms. Finally, all desire and longing will have to grow into love. In the struggle that this path implies a new encounter with Christianity will become possible — an encounter that leads out of loneliness into the community of men and the cosmos.

We ourselves will have to follow this path, over the threshold of day-consciousness into the totally conscious night-consciousness. It is a path of concentration and meditation, of open-mindedness and tolerance, of courage and trust in the hand that will be stretched out to us from the other side of the threshold.

A healthy path of development can only be travelled in the balance of the path outwards and the path inwards, in that order. For on the outward path thought is strengthened in such a way that it can stand up to overwhelming experiences on the inward path.

Going over the threshold *outwards* leads to a new spiritual science, a new medicine, a new agriculture. Going over the threshold *inwards* leads to a new spiritual anthropology, a new pedagogy, a new psychiatry. Both paths together lead to a new social science in which the concept of development is crucial, a development that becomes visible in the biography of the single individual and in society. This social development has led us once again into a critical phase. The real problem here is *not* how the greatest possible material prosperity may be most fairly distributed; the real problem is whether we have the courage to push through from materialism into a new spiritual realism. It is only from here that material problems can be tackled in a new, different and better way.

Recommended Reading

Adler, A., *Individual Psychology of Alfred Adler* (New York, 1956).

——, *Die Technik der Individualpsychologie*, I and II (Munich, 1928–30).

Allport, G. W., *Becoming* (New Haven, 1955).

Andriessen, H. C. J., *Groei en grens in de volwassenheid* (Nijmegen, 1970).

Assagioli, R., *The Act of Will* (New York, 1973).

——, *Psychosynthesis. A Manual of Principles and Techniques* (New York, 1974).

Bergler, E., *The Revolt of the Middle-aged Man* (New York, 1954).

——, *De illusie van de tweede jeugd* (Amsterdam, 1956).

Blauner, R., *Alienation and Freedom* (Chicago, 1970).

Bovet, Th., *Führung durch die Lebensalter* (Bern, 1955).

Bühler, Ch., *Der menschliche Lebenslauf als psychologisches Problem* (Göttingen, 1959).

Buytendijk, F. J. J., *Mens en dier* (Utrecht, 1972).

Chorus, A. M. J., *Psychologie van de menselijke levensloop. Hoofdstukken ener ontwikkelingspsychologie* (Leiden, 1959).

Ciba Congress, *Man and His Future* (London, 1963).

Cole, L., and Hall, J. M., *The Psychology of Adolescence* (New York, 1964).

Dewey, J., *Experience and Education* (London, 1965).

Dreikers, R. A., *Adler Individualpsychologie* (Rotterdam, 1933).

Erikson, E. H., 'Das Problem der Identität', *Psyche*, 1956–57, 1–3/X.

——, *Wachstum und Krisen der gesunden Persönlichkeit* (Stuttgart, 1953).

Evans, R. I., *Conversations with Carl Jung* (New York, 1964).

Frankl, V. E., *The Doctor and the Soul. From Psychotherapy to Logotherapy* (New York, 1973).

——, *Homo Patiens* (Vienna, 1950).

Freud, S., *Civilization and Its Discontents* (New York, 1962).

——, *Psychoanalyse* (Amsterdam, 1955).

Goethe, J. W. von, *(Glückliches Ereignis in der) Metamorphose der Pflanzen.*

Guardini, R., *Die Lebensalter: ihre ethische und pädagogische Bedeulung* (Würzburg, 1957).

Harris, D., *The Concept of Development. An Issue in Study of Human Behavior* (Minneapolis, 1957).

Hemleben, J., *Rudolf Steiner. A Documentary Biography* (East Grinstead, 1976).

Hillenius, D., in *N. R. C.-Handelsblad*, 16. 6. 1973.

Hoffman, B., *The Tyranny of Testing* (New York, 1962).

Humboldt-Gesellschaft, *Das Menschenbild der Gegenwart* (Mannheim, 1964).

Jaffé, A., *Jung over parapsychologie en alchemie* (Rotterdam, 1975).

——, *Der Mythus vom Sinn im Werk von C. G. Jung* (Zürich, 1967).

Jung, C. G., *Man and His Symbols* (New York, 1968).

——, *Memories, Dreams, Reflections* (New York, 1965).

Kaufmann, R., *De mensenmakers* (Amsterdam, 1965).

Künkel, H., *Die Lebensalter* (Konstanz, 1957)

Laing, R. D., *Strategie van de ervaring* (Meppel, 1969).

Lauer, H. E., *Der menschliche Lebenslauf* (Freiburg i. Br., 1952).

Leent, J. A. A. van, *Sociale psychologie in drie dimensies* (Utrecht, 1961).

Lewin, K., art. in Cartwright and Zander, *Group Dynamics* (New York, 1953).

Lievegoed, B. C. J., *The Developing Organization* (London, 1973).

——, *Ontwikkelingsfasen van het kind* (Zeist, 1946, 1974).

Lievense, J., *Je rijpt je rot* (Amsterdam, 1975).

Maslow, A. H., *Motivation and Personality*, 2nd ed. (New York, 1970).

——, *Religions, Values and Peak Experience* (Columbus, 1964).

——, *Toward a Psychology of Being*, 2nd ed. (New York, 1968).

McGregor, D., *The Human Side of Enterprise* (New York, 1960).

Moers, M., *Die Entwicklungsphasen des menschlichen Lebens* (Ratingen, 1953).

——, *Das weibliche Seelenbeden* (Bonn, 1950).

Morris, D., *The Naked Ape* (New York, 1969).

Neumann, E., *Dieptepsychologie en nieuwe ethiek* (Arnhem, 1959).

Parker, E., *The Seven Ages of Woman* (Baltimore, 1960).

Peter, J., Laurens and R. Hull, *The Peter Principle* (New York, 1969).

Portmann, A., *Zoologie und das Bild des Menschen* (Reinbek, 1959).

Post, L. van der, *Jung and the Story of Our time* (New York, 1975).

Roethlisberger, F. J., *Management and the Worker* (Cambridge, Mass., 1950).

Rogers, C. R., *Psychotherapy and Personality Change* (Chicago, 1954).

Rümke, H. C., *Levenstijdperken van de man* (Amsterdam, 1963).

Schiller, F., *Briefe über die aesthetische Erziehung des Menschen*.

Siroka, R. W., *Sensitivity Training and Group Encounter* (New York).

Skinner, B. F., *Beyond Freedom and Dignity* (New York, 1971).

Steiner, R., *Knowledge of the Higher Worlds – How Is It Achieved?* 6th ed. (London, 1976).

——, *Occult Science – an Outline* (London, 1979).

——, *The Philosophy of Freedom* (London, 1979).

——, *Theory of Knowledge Implicit in Goethe's World-Conception* (London, 1940).

——, *Theosophy* (London, 1973).

Strasser, S., *Fenomenologie en empirische menskunde* (Arnhem, 1962).

Trimbos, K., *Antipsychiatrie* (Deventer, 1975).

Verbrugh, H. S., *Geneeskunde op dood spoor* (Rotterdam, 1974).

Watzlawick, P., Weakland & Fisch, *Het kan anders* (Deventer, 1974).

Watson, J. B., *Behaviourism*, 2nd ed. (London, 1931).

Wehr, G., C. G. *Jung in Selbstzeugnissen und Bilddokumenten* (Reinbek, 1970).

Wijngaarden, H. R., *Hoofdproblemen der volwassenheid* (Utrecht, 1950).